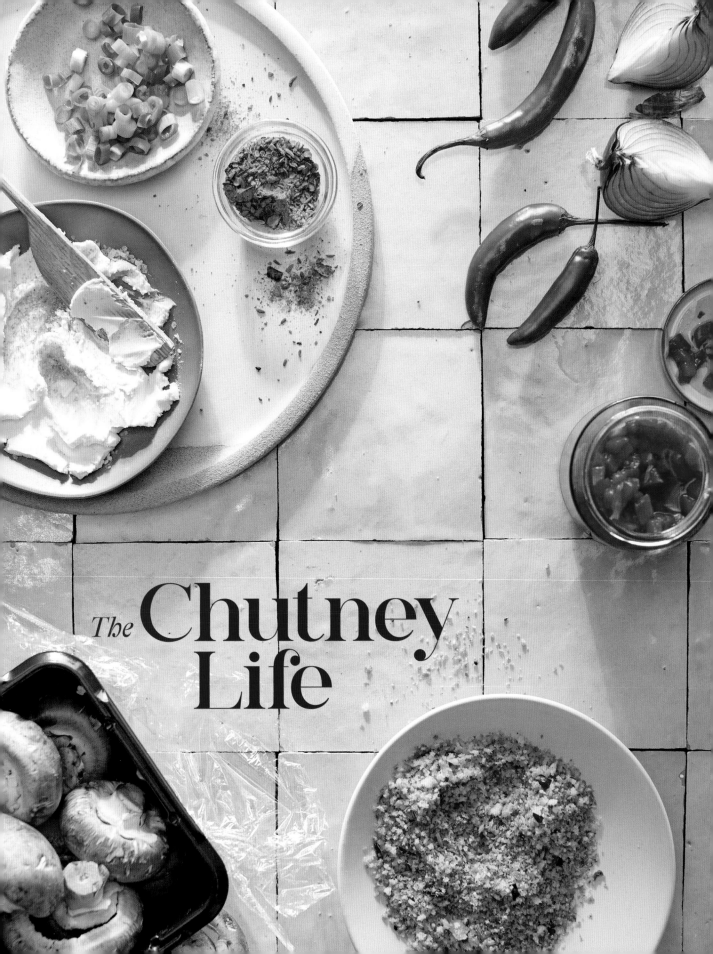

The Chutney Life

The Chutney Life

100 Easy-to-Make Indian-Inspired Recipes

Palak Patel

Photographs by Emily Dorio

ABRAMS, NEW YORK

Editor: Holly Dolce
Designer: Laura Palese
Design Manager: Darilyn Lowe Carnes
Managing Editor: Annalea Manalili
Production Manager: Kathleen Gaffney

Library of Congress Control Number: 2023932420

ISBN: 978-1-4197-6439-4
eISBN: 979-8-88707-189-3

Printed and bound in China
10 9 8 7 6 5 4 3 2 1

Abrams books are available at special discounts when
purchased in quantity for premiums and promotions
as well as fundraising or educational use. Special
editions can also be created to specification. For
details, contact specialsales@abramsbooks.com or
the address below.

Abrams® is a registered trademark of
Harry N. Abrams, Inc.

ABRAMS The Art of Books
195 Broadway, New York, NY 10007
abramsbooks.com

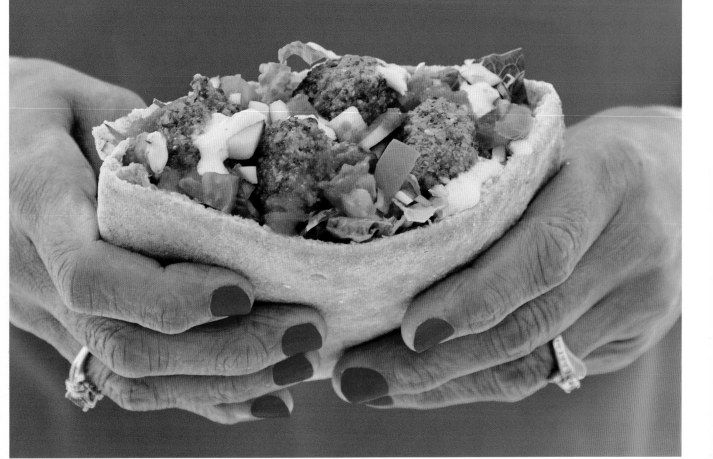

FOR MY MOM,
whose loving hands
raised and fed me

LAMB KHEEMA–STUFFED
PEPPERS (PAGE 150)

INTRODUCTION

About This Book . . .

The Chutney Life is so many things—a tribute to the nostalgic foods I grew up eating, an extension of *The Chutney Life* blog, and a look inside my blended Indian American experience. While my roots are Gujarati, and both of my parents are from the state of Gujarat, I was born and raised in Philadelphia, the City of Brotherly Love, and, yes, the home of the best cheesesteaks and soft pretzels IN. THE. WORLD. In many ways, you could say I've lived the typical immigrant experience. My parents came to America in the mid-eighties, worked multiple jobs, learned English as best they could, and sacrificed a lot of their time and effort to provide a better life for my brother and me. My childhood was wholesome, surrounded by cousins and (loud) aunts and uncles at weekly family gatherings in our homes. It is this joyful chaos that is the crux of my being.

For years we lived in a joint family home (seventeen of us at one point!). Having so many people under one roof meant that there was pretty much never any peace and quiet. But it also meant there was always lots of food, which always brought us together. If the women in the family weren't in the kitchen cooking, they'd be on the floor, sitting on a bedsheet, splaying out bunches and bunches of fresh cilantro to dry, or peeling mountains of garlic for the next day. The food scene was always poppin' in the Patel household.

Each day I would come home from school knowing we'd be having rotli dal bhaat shaak (dubbed RDBS by my generation) for dinner. I see now that this was my parents' way of preserving our culture, hanging on to something that often felt so far away. But I won't lie, like your typical child and teenager, I didn't always love these traditional meals. Eventually my mom gave in and tried her best to make us more "American" foods like pasta and grilled cheese sandwiches—but always with her little desi mom touch. She'd make sandwiches out of leftover shaak or whatever vegetable dish we had left over from the night before with a spread of chutney, or whip up a quick spaghetti with some sautéed mustard seeds and jalapeños to jazz up a jarred pasta sauce. Eventually her confidence in the kitchen and vast experience with spices and flavor combinations led her to make fusion meals before fusion was even a thing! Whipping up falafel and enchiladas for dinner, like it was no big deal. I call her the OG food blogger.

There is so much of my mom in me that I am so drawn to, inspired by, and eager to share with the world, especially her experimental intuition when it comes to cooking. Honoring both parts of my identity has translated into the way I cook. While I love traditional Gujarati dishes like bataka poha and dangela, I also love me some tacos for dinner, or french toast for breakfast, because guess what? Indian people eat more than Indian food!

The recipes you'll find in this book are a true reflection of my experience growing up in America, surrounded by so many different cultural influences, communities, and the food that I've eaten along the way. You'll see a lot of Mexican inspiration in this book, including chilaquiles, enchiladas, and tacos, because Mexican and Indian food have parallel flavor profiles, including their heavy use of chiles, cilantro, and cumin. And both cuisines offer tons of vegetarian options. In contrast, you'll also find recipes for many of the classic dishes that I might have taken a pass on when I was growing up, but that I now crave (yes, Mom, you were right)! A comforting and cozy bowl of dal fry or a recipe for chaat to spruce up a Friday night dinner is sometimes just what I need.

The recipes in *The Chutney Life* reflect the way I live. On busy weeknights, you're likely to find me scarfing down a Samosa Grilled Cheese (page 109) with one hand and wrangling a rowdy toddler with the other. On weekends, I may tackle more complex and time-consuming recipes, such as Lamb Kheema–Stuffed Peppers (page 150) or Paneer Makhni (page 156), or something more elegant like Panko-Crusted Halibut with Jammy Harissa Tomatoes (page 201).

My goal in writing this book is to offer recipes and techniques that capture the intricacies of Indian cooking, but also present them in a way that is realistic and attainable for home cooks. To help with this, I've included "Pro Tips" throughout the book—tricks and hacks to save you time and effort, plus plenty of recommendations for simple ingredient swaps to make a dish more to your personal taste. Don't like feta? Swap it out for cheddar. Cauliflower not your thing? Try roasted sweet potatoes instead. And when it comes to heat and chiles, while I like to amp it up—the quantities called for in these recipes are fairly spicy—you may want to take it down a notch, or even crank it up some. Finally, with the exception of the "Non-Veg" chapter, most of the recipes in this book are vegetarian, but you can add chicken or another meat to many of the recipes, if desired. The same can be said for swapping out some of the animal proteins for chickpeas, beans, or tofu in the non-veg recipes offered here. I'm all about encouraging you to customize these dishes to your own liking.

I created these recipes for people like me—busy, resourceful home cooks who want the effort they put into shopping, prepping, and cooking a dish to be well worth it. I've provided a spice and pantry guide in the front of this book, along with explanations about ingredients and recipe titles in the headnotes, but feel free to Google terms you may be unfamiliar with to get more context.

It is my hope that through these recipes you find joy in embracing the magic of flavors that transcend time and tradition, and in meals that are celebratory, unique, and keep you on your toes!

Meet the Family . . .

You'll see a lot of faces in this book—family, friends, or as I like to say, *framily*, sprinkled throughout. My tiny little *nuclear family* unit consists of my husband, Pinank, and my two boys, Shaan, who is the eldest, and Sahil. But *immediate family* is a loosely used term in my culture! My parents live a little over an hour away but visit often, and my in-laws live across the street (yup, it's an *Everybody Loves Raymond* situation but with way more privacy, so it's all good!). My brother and his wife had their baby boy, Niam, just one day before I had Sahil, and we get together often, usually opting to stay in and have dinner or brunch together so the kids can run around and we can hang, worry-free. Pinank's sister and her husband live in LA and visit for the big holidays, so it's always fun to cook up a big feast when they're in town. My masi, Mom's sister, Guddi, whom I like to call "My Fun Mom," has lived with my family since she was a teenager. Her kids, Dev and Chandani, who you see in my Instagram Stories as they've lived with me on and off over the years, are my official taste testers and basically my first-born children. This tight-knit crew makes up my "immediate family," and this entire book was written while keeping their food preferences in mind, because that's how I've always cooked and hosted. I always want there to be something for everyone. And with these recipes, you'll find dozens of options for putting together a menu perfect for hosting your in-laws for lunch or your friends for drinks and dinner. The combinations are endless!

I've been known to say that I don't really love to cook . . . but I absolutely *love* to feed people. It's how I show my love. No matter the occasion, food helps translate our sentiments and emotions into delicious and nourishing little morsels of comfort for ourselves, and for those we love.

Guide to Indian Spices

Below is a list of spices that are used in recipes throughout *The Chutney Life*. You may not be familiar with all of them, but chances are good you'll be using most of them as you cook your way through this book. Most supermarkets will carry spices like ground cumin and coriander, but you will likely need to visit your local South Asian market to find some of the less commonly found spices. I promise it will be worth the trip, as they will be less expensive and fresher than what might be sitting on supermarket shelves. If you've never been to a South Asian market, give yourself a stretch of time to wander the aisles, take in all of the offerings, and ask questions! Here, you will find traditional spices and sweeteners including hing (asafetida) and jaggery, and lentils such as split urad dal, dry white peas, and more. If you don't have a South Asian market near you, most of these items can be bought online. Two of my favorite retailers are shopindianeats.com and diasporaco.com. Penzey's spices (penzeys.com) is a great resource for stocking your spice cabinet with everyday spices such as garlic powder, cinnamon, and peppercorns. Generally, I don't keep spices for longer than a year. If their color or aroma starts to fade, I know it's time to replace them.

ACHAR MASALA

This puckery Indian pickling spice blend combines more than a dozen spices, including mustard seed, fenugreek, cumin, turmeric, and mango powder. In addition to using it for pickling, I love using it to jazz up boiled eggs!

AJWAIN SEEDS

I like to rub these sharp, slightly bitter seeds between my hands before adding them to a recipe to release their strong oils and essence, which is similar to thyme.

AMCHUR POWDER

Made from unripe mangoes that are dried and ground, this tangy powder can be added to a variety of dishes, including chutneys, curries, dal, and even some fruit, and is used much like citrus zest.

BLACK SALT

This pungent salt is complex: It smells slightly of sulfur and adds a deeper layer of flavor to dishes. It's potent even when called for in tiny amounts. It is a must-have!

GROUND CARDAMOM

Cardamom is part of the ginger family. It's often combined with nutmeg and cinnamon and used for both baking and cooking. It's the special little touch in my Banana-Cardamom Crumb Muffins (page 45).

CHAAT MASALA BLEND

A spice blend used to add flavor to chaat, sandwiches, and meats. It is made up of a variety of spices, including cumin, coriander, amchur, ginger, black salt, and red chili powder.

CORIANDER SEEDS/GROUND CORIANDER

You'll see ground coriander called for in many recipes, and in our home, we use a blend of ground coriander and cumin, also called dhana jeera powder, which you can find at almost any South Asian market or online. You can make a similar blend by dry roasting coriander and cumin seeds (about 80:20 percent ratio of coriander to cumin), then grinding in a spice grinder. Using just ground coriander is fine, too. To make ground coriander from whole seeds, just toast them, let them cool, and then grind in a spice grinder.

CUMIN SEEDS/GROUND CUMIN

Probably my favorite whole spice, this nutty seed is found in Indian curries and chutneys, rice dishes, soups, and more. Like coriander, cumin seeds' flavor is enhanced when toasted and then combined with hot oil before adding additional ingredients, to help flavor the dish.

FRESH CURRY LEAVES

These vibrant green leaves lend a fresh, slightly bitter, citrusy quality to dishes. Add them to curries and dals when you incorporate other spices or chop them finely and add them to chutneys.

FENNEL SEEDS

These seeds have a distinct earthy, licorice-like flavor. They can be used to enhance vegetable dishes, meat, chutneys, and more. Gently crushing them and tossing into chai is also a fave!

GARAM MASALA

This spice blend is widely used in Indian cooking. While its composition varies by region, it generally tends to be some combination of black pepper, cardamom, cinnamon, clove, cumin, and red chili powder. It's usually added to dishes right before serving, so the spices remain bold and fragrant. It can also vary greatly by brand and region, and I've found that packaged chole masala provides a very similar flavor profile.

HING (ASAFETIDA)

This pungent, sulfur-like spice has hints of onion and leek and works to bring out the flavor and intensity of all of the other spices it gets combined with.

JAGGERY

Used as a sweetener in many traditional Indian dishes, jaggery provides the caramel flavors reminiscent of brown sugar. It is light brown and comes in a smooth, hard block. You shave bits off with a paring knife, and it quickly melts and combines into a dish. If you do not have jaggery, you can use white or packed brown sugar in most recipes that call for it.

MUSTARD SEEDS

Commonly found in Indian cooking, when these bitter seeds are added to a hot pan of oil they deliver extra flavor and texture to any dish. They are the star in my Spaghetti Squash Masala (page 126) and their ground version provides the zing to my Athela Marcha (page 264).

RED CHILI POWDER

When it comes to Indian cooking, there are a TON of different chili powders to choose from. Some, like kashmiri chili powder, are used mainly to impart color and minimal heat. Others, like dyagi, can vary in their heat and flavor profiles. I like to have two, one that gives a great deep color and one that brings the heat. I often blend the two together for a dish.

STAR ANISE

This licorice-like dried herb can be used whole or ground. It enhances flavors in Chinese, Vietnamese, Indian, and Middle Eastern cuisines. It pairs especially well with rich meats, can be mulled in wine, or used for a chutney.

TANDOORI MASALA

With its ginger, garlic, and fenugreek, this spice blend is similar in flavor to garam masala (see opposite) but is traditionally added as part of a marinade, rather than after the dish is cooked. I prefer Swad brand, which is what I use in my Tandoori Onion Tart (page 238).

THECHA

This spicy, flavorful chutney-like condiment combines chiles, garlic, cumin seeds, and salt into a paste that I use in so many ways that I've pretty much lost count! It's tasty mixed into cream cheese or mayo as a spread, or drop a bit into soup to up the spice quotient. I add it to any dish when I want to raise the heat level!

GROUND TURMERIC

This earthy spice, with its rich yellow color, is probably the most popular of dry Indian spices because of all its health benefits. While it's added in rather small quantities to most dishes in this book, it's still vital to any dish it lends its flavor to!

Stock Up for Your Chutney Life!

Unlike today, back when I was growing up, my mom never shopped for groceries multiple times a week. Instead, a practiced bargain hunter, she'd carefully study the weekly supermarket circulars, and when sales were on, we'd stock up on everything from canned beans to cooking oil to paper goods. We also drove a couple hours to Edison, New Jersey, a few times a year to stock up on Indian pantry essentials because we didn't always have a local option. This way, when we wanted to make something on a whim, we always had the ingredients on hand! Below are some of the most frequently used items found in my pantry that will be super helpful in working your way through this book. My mom would be proud if you keep them at the ready!

GRAINS, LEGUMES, AND LENTILS

Basmati rice

Quinoa

Urad dal

Chana dal

Toor dal

Canned black beans

Canned chickpeas

Canned kidney beans

Dry white peas

Kala chana (black chickpeas)

Peanuts (raw and unsalted)

Sesame seeds

MISCELLANEOUS

Flour tortillas

Corn tortillas

Naan

Burrata

Roti (frozen)

All-purpose flour

Vegetable broth

Canned coconut milk

Frozen samosas

Papdi

Puri

CONDIMENTS

Tomato paste

Canned tomato sauce

Jarred marinara sauce

Honey

Rice wine vinegar

Apple cider vinegar

Soy sauce

Harissa

Extra-virgin olive oil

Neutral oils (canola and vegetable)

Prepared barbecue sauce
   (I like Sweet Baby Ray's)

Hoisin sauce

Mayonnaise

Dijon mustard

Pickled jalapeños

Chipotle in adobo sauce

Tahini

Apple butter

Gochujang (Korean chili paste)

Sriracha sauce

A Guide to Green Chiles

The recipes in this book bring some heat! While I recommend using the specified type of green chiles noted in each recipe, I understand that not everyone's heat tolerance is the same, so feel free to crank it up or tone it down. If a recipe calls for Thai green chiles and you are more of a moderate heat person, swap them out for serranos. That said, it's important to note that chiles not only impart spiciness, they also lend important flavor to a wide variety of dishes.

One thing to be aware of when you're trying to figure out how much heat to bring to a dish is how the chiles will be used in a recipe. Different preparations affect the level of heat the chiles give off. So, while one serrano, finely diced, is plenty for roughly 1 cup (240 ml) chimichurri sauce, six serranos, blended into the batter for dangela (page 38), which yields almost 6 cups (1.4 L) of a rice- and lentil-based batter, would not deliver enough heat (trust me, I've experimented).

One other variable when it comes to chiles is the seeds. Most of the heat from chiles is located in the seeds and the white interior membrane that surrounds them. Growing up, we never seeded or cored our green chiles. However, if you want to lessen the level of heat in a dish, remove the seeds and membrane before chopping the pepper.

As you make the recipes in this book again and again, you'll be able to get a true sense of what your personal heat preference is, and how to modify the type and amount of chiles to hit your spicy target. You may even find yourself ordering "Indian Hot" the next time you're at your local Indian restaurant!

The recipes on the pages that follow generally call for the following types of green chiles (in order from mild to hot):

POBLANOS

While I'd never use these for spice, I do love their taste, and they are perfect for roasting or grilling and stuffing. They are a must for my poblano cream sauce (see page 142) or Chilaquiles Verdes with Esquites (page 31) and Lamb Kheema–Stuffed Peppers (page 150)!

JALAPEÑOS

These medium-size (2- to 3-inch long/5 to 7.5 cm) firm, dark green chiles can be found in most supermarkets. I love jalapeños for their flavor profile, which to me is similar to a fiery green bell pepper. But don't be fooled . . . some varieties of jalapeños can really be spicy. Slice them thinly and add them to anything from salsa to pizza to eggs. Jalapeños and cilantro pair perfectly together, as you can taste in my Cilantro Jalapeño Sauce (page 252) or Cilantro Jalapeño Hummus (page 237).

SERRANOS

I find these bright chiles to be the most versatile of the chiles listed here. They are the perfect compromise between mild and hot. They are usually green, but can also be red. They are smaller than jalapeños, and tend to be 2 to 4 times hotter. You'll find them in so many of my recipes, including Crispy Gochujang-Glazed Sweet Potato Tacos (page 136) and Mom's Falafel (page 146), which calls for 15 to 20 of these babies!

THAI GREEN CHILES

These chiles hit a high note when it comes to heat. Super spicy, they are popular in both Southeast Asian and South American cuisines. I find them to also be the most consistent and reliable when it comes to spice level, as they are always, always spicy! They add both depth and heat to Lamb Kheema–Stuffed Peppers (page 150) and Kasturi Onion Bhajiya (page 186).

Essential Tools and Equipment for TCL

When it comes to tools and equipment, I try to only keep on hand the items I feel are essential to the way I cook. I hate buying something because it looks or sounds cool, only to realize later that it takes up too much space or I never use it. The items listed below are the workhorses of my kitchen that I use throughout the week.

FOOD PROCESSOR
(mini and regular) with shredding and slicing attachments
This machine takes most of the work out of the prep for everything from slaws to hash browns, to sauces and salsas. I use the full-size one for falafel batter, and love the mini version for mincing garlic, ginger, green chiles, and more. It is also what I use to make almost all of my sauces, including Cilantro Jalapeño Sauce (page 252).

SPICE GRINDER
A few of the recipes in this book call for making your own spice blend, which is best when you toast whole spices and then blend them together in a spice grinder. I usually don't buy already ground spices, like ground cumin; instead I toast the cumin seeds and then grind them for a richer, stronger, fresher flavor.

MICROPLANE GRATER
This handy tool is perfect for grating a few garlic cloves or fresh ginger, turning it into a paste-like consistency that allows it to blend more seamlessly into whatever you are making. It also makes zesting citrus or grating fresh nutmeg a breeze. And it's perfect for grating fresh Pecorino Romano over pretty much anything—my obsession!

HIGH-SPEED BLENDER
This is a must for items like Cilantro Chutney (page 193), which is made in a big batch, and for grinding batters that consist of rice and lentils, like dangela and uttapam. You cannot replace a blender with a food processor or hand mixer, as they will not be able to deliver the same texture and consistency.

CAST-IRON SKILLET OR NONSTICK SKILLET

A well-seasoned cast-iron pan offers a natural nonstick coating. A nonstick skillet offers a similar surface without the extra weight. Both are ideal for making dangela (page 38), uttapam (page 165), and Masoor Dal Pudla (page 172). These items will simply not work in a stainless-steel skillet.

DUTCH OVEN OR HEAVY-BOTTOMED POT

Most of my soups are made in a sturdy dutch oven or heavy-bottomed pot. Invest in quality for these pots, as you will be cooking low and slow in these.

GLASS OR CERAMIC BAKING DISH (9 by 13 inches/ 23 by 33 cm)

From stuffed peppers to enchiladas to brownies, this standard-size baking dish will be on heavy rotation as the baking vessel of choice in your kitchen.

BAKING SHEET PANS

I like to have three or four of these rimmed aluminum baking sheets on hand for various kitchen prep—both the half sheet size (13 by 18 inches/33 by 46 cm) and quarter sheet size (9½ by 13 inches/24 by 33 cm). I roast everything on them, from chicken to vegetables. I use them to freeze fruit, bake cookies, you name it.

BHARELA RINGAN & BATAKA, PAGE 167

BREAKFAST & BRUNCH

It's 6:00 a.m. on a typical weekday morning. My brother and I are in middle school, and one of us is likely eating Eggo waffles drenched in syrup, while the other is happily bent over a bowl of cereal, Fruity Pebbles or Trix—only the good stuff, of course. My mom, on the other hand, is probably halfway through making a full, traditional Gujarati meal of rotli, dal, shaak, and rice, a portion of which she will pack up for my dad's lunch and her own. Again, I repeat, it's just 6:00 a.m. With both of my parents working multiple jobs, my mom needs to spend her time wisely. So, like the superwoman she is, she'll have lunch and dinner ready before the day even starts.

The breakfasts I make now, as an adult, look a lot different. In this book, you'll find that I've amped up the flavor in brunch and breakfast recipes (and pretty much everything I make!) with Indian spices and ingredients, which will no doubt surprise and hopefully inspire you to do the same. My Banana-Cardamom Crumb Muffins (page 45) are generously spiced with cardamom, the quintessential ingredient in many Indian desserts. My Turkish-inspired eggs (page 36) get some earthiness from cumin and coriander. And while my cereal obsession has not ended, I've found with a little prep and planning, a wholesome breakfast on a weekday morning isn't completely off the table. Breakfast Naan Pizza (page 35), Overnight Mango Chia Pudding (page 50), and Tahini, Coffee & Chickoo Shake (page 54) are handy because they won't leave behind a pile of dishes. When you have more time to prep, or want to celebrate a special occasion, invite your nearest and dearest to a weekend brunch where you'll impress them with Baked French Toast with Whipped Raspberry-Rose Yogurt (page 28), Chilaquiles Verdes with Esquites (page 31), and Asparagus & Pepper Jack Rosti with Tarragon Garlic Aioli (page 42).

Whether you're looking for a quick breakfast that helps get you out the door in the morning or brunch ideas to help you and yours kick back and relax over the weekend, this chapter guarantees the perfect recipes!

BAKED FRENCH TOAST

with WHIPPED RASPBERRY-ROSE YOGURT

Serves 6

1 cup packed (220 g) brown sugar

¾ teaspoon ground cardamom

½ teaspoon ground cinnamon

1 cup (130 g) unsalted pistachios, finely chopped

2 large eggs

4 large egg yolks

1 teaspoon vanilla extract

2 tablespoons plus 2 teaspoons rose water

½ teaspoon salt

2½ cups (600 ml) half-and-half

8 strands or 2 large pinches saffron

1 (14-ounce/400 g) loaf brioche or challah, cut into 1-inch (2.5 cm) chunks

½ cup (120 ml) full-fat plain Greek yogurt

2 tablespoons cream cheese

¼ cup (60 ml) raspberry jam

½ cup (120 ml) heavy cream

1 cup (125 g) fresh raspberries, for garnish

PRO TIP

The whipped yogurt topping, which adds a tart, bright, and just a little bit bougie note, is best made right before you serve it. If you need to make it ahead and refrigerate it, be sure to give it another quick whip just before serving. You can also freeze this to enjoy as a frozen yogurt treat anytime!

This reminds me of a warm, comforting, custardy bread pudding. The top layer gets this beautiful nutty crunch from the brown sugar and pistachios, while the saffron- and cream-soaked challah underneath it all is pillowy soft. It's the dish that steals the spotlight when you set it on the table, so be prepared for all the oohs and ahhs! This is a convenient dish to serve to a crowd because you can prep it ahead of time, then pop it in the fridge for a couple of hours and bake it right before guests are due to arrive. It's a showstopper that will have everyone singing your praises!

Butter a 9 by 13–inch (23 by 33 cm) baking dish.

In a small bowl, mix together the brown sugar, cardamom, cinnamon, and pistachios. Set aside ¼ cup for the topping.

In a large bowl, lightly whisk the eggs and egg yolks. Add the vanilla, 2 tablespoons of the rose water, salt, 2¼ cups (540 ml) of the half-and-half, and the remaining sugar and pistachio mixture to the eggs and whisk to combine.

In a small bowl, microwave the remaining ¼ cup (60 ml) half-and-half for 20 seconds, or until warm. Add the saffron and stir to release the fragrance. Lightly whisk the saffron-infused half-and-half into the egg mixture.

Add the bread to the prepared pan and pour the egg mixture evenly over the top, gently pressing the bread down to fully absorb the mixture. Cover tightly with foil and refrigerate for 20 minutes, or up to 3 hours.

About 15 minutes before you're ready to bake the french toast, preheat the oven to 350°F (175°C).

Bake covered for 30 minutes, then remove the foil and sprinkle with the reserved sugar and pistachio topping. Bake until the top is golden brown, about 15 minutes more.

While the french toast is baking, make the whipped raspberry-rose yogurt. Place the yogurt, cream cheese, jam, and remaining 2 teaspoons rose water in a chilled bowl. Using a handheld mixer, beat on medium-high speed until smooth, 1 to 2 minutes. Add the heavy cream and whip on high speed for about 2 minutes more, just until the mixture looks like soft clouds; take care not to overwhip.

Slice the french toast into 6 portions and serve each portion immediately with a dollop of the whipped yogurt and some raspberries on top.

CHILAQUILES *VERDES*

with ESQUITES

Serves 4

For the tortilla chips

- About ¼ cup (60 ml) canola or vegetable oil
- 8 corn tortillas, quartered (or more if you prefer lots of chips)
- Coarse sea salt

For the street corn salad

- 3 cups (435 g) cooked corn kernels
- ⅓ cup (40 g) Cotija cheese
- 2 cups (480 ml) mayonnaise
- 1½ teaspoons ancho chili powder or chipotle chili powder
- 2 tablespoons plus 1½ teaspoons fresh lime juice
- Pinch salt

Chilaquiles are fried, saucy tortillas topped with eggs and toppings. And I love all things verde, so I used lots of zippy tomatillos, cilantro, and jalapeños to achieve a nice green salsa, and then topped everything off with esquites, the most addictive Mexican street corn salad. While these chilaquiles aren't necessarily quick and easy, the chips, salsa, and street corn can all be made a few days in advance, so it's just a matter of assembling and heating before you're ready to dig in! While I like to lightly pan-fry the corn tortillas in a skillet to get them crisp and bring out their aroma, you can take a shortcut and buy premade tortilla chips; just be sure to look for the thicker, home-style variety so they will hold up to the salsa.

MAKE THE TORTILLA CHIPS: Line a plate with paper towels.

Heat a large skillet over medium-high heat, add 1 tablespoon of the oil, and place as many of the tortilla pieces as you can fit in a single layer. Cook until crisp, 2 to 3 minutes, turning once, until the chips are golden brown on both sides. Transfer the chips to the plate with the paper towels and sprinkle with coarse sea salt while the chips are still hot. Repeat, adding additional oil as necessary, a tablespoon at a time, until all of the tortillas are crisp.

MAKE THE STREET CORN: Add the corn kernels, cheese, mayonnaise, chili powder, lime juice, and salt to a bowl and toss to combine.

continues

For the salsa verde

- 3 pounds (1.4 kg) tomatillos, husks removed, washed and halved
- 2 jalapeño chiles, seeded and roughly chopped
- 2 poblano chiles, seeded and roughly chopped
- 2 white onions, peeled and quartered

  Salt
- 1 cup tightly packed (40 g) roughly chopped fresh cilantro (leaves and tender stems)
- 8 large cloves garlic, peeled
- 1 teaspoon ground cumin
- 3 teaspoons fresh lime juice

For the assembly and garnishes

- ½ cup (1 stick/115 g) unsalted butter
- 8 fried eggs (see Pro Tip)
- 3 tablespoons thinly sliced green onions
- ¼ cup (25 g) thinly sliced radishes
- ¼ cup (30 g) thinly sliced red onions
- ¼ cup (25 g) Cotija cheese

PRO TIP

Everyone makes their fried eggs differently, but here's how I like mine: Melt butter (1 tablespoon per egg) in a nonstick pan set over medium-high heat, then add two large eggs per person. As the eggs start to set, after 2 to 3 minutes, pierce each yolk so it spreads and cooks a bit, then cover the pan and continue to cook for an additional 2 to 3 minutes, so the eggs steam but don't develop crispy edges. If you're a fan of crispy edges, don't cover the pan.

MAKE THE SALSA VERDE: Add the tomatillos, jalapeños, poblanos, onions, and a pinch of salt to a stockpot. Cover with water and bring to a boil over high heat. Cover, lower the heat to a simmer, and cook for about 10 minutes, until the onions are softened and translucent. Drain the cooked tomatillo mixture and transfer the solids to a blender. Allow the mixture to cool until it is just warm, and then add the cilantro, garlic, cumin, 2½ teaspoons salt, and the lime juice. Pulse until the mixture is mostly smooth with a few small chunks remaining.

ASSEMBLE THE CHILAQUILES: Melt the butter in a large skillet over medium heat. Add the salsa, stir, and add the fried tortilla chips. (If your skillet isn't large enough, you can do this in batches.) Toss gently to quickly coat the chips in the salsa and transfer to 4 individual plates or one large serving plate. Top each serving with two fried eggs and a few spoonfuls of the street corn, and garnish with the green onions, radishes, red onions, and a sprinkle of Cotija cheese. Or assemble all of the components on a single platter. Serve warm.

Breakfast
NAAN PIZZA

Serves 4

For the salsa

- 2 cups (360 g) chopped cherry tomatoes
- ¼ cup (10 g) finely chopped fresh cilantro
- 1 tablespoon extra-virgin olive oil
- Juice of ½ lime, plus more if needed
- ½ teaspoon salt, plus more if needed
- ½ teaspoon ground cumin

For the pizza

- 1 (8-ounce/225 g) package cream cheese (I prefer Philadelphia brand)
- 2½ to 3 tablespoons prepared thecha chutney or Lasaynu Marchu (page 263)
- 3 to 4 tablespoons unsalted butter, softened
- 4 large naan or 8 mini naan (see Note)
- 8 large eggs
- 2 ripe avocados, pitted and thinly sliced
- Salt and freshly ground black pepper
- 4 lime wedges

NOTE

Because these pizzas are more filling than they look, I make them on mini naan if I can find them, as they're perfect for a serving with just one egg on top!

I will essentially eat anything if you serve it to me on top of a warm, soft, buttery piece of naan. These breakfast naan pizzas have been a staple in our home for years, mainly because of how simple and easy they are to make. Because I loathe doing dishes, I usually toast up all the naan first, and then wipe down the skillet and fry the eggs in the same pan—efficiency, people. The star of this dish is hands down the cream cheese layer made with Lasanyu Marchu (page 263). I have a tub of this premade in my fridge at all times, as it is such a flavorful and versatile condiment. The tomato salsa really brings some zip to these pizzas, too. But if I'm being honest, on weekdays I skip the salsa just so I don't have to wash a cutting board, and the pizzas are still incredibly satisfying!

Preheat the oven to 200°F (90°C)

MAKE THE SALSA: Mix the tomatoes, cilantro, olive oil, lime juice, salt, and cumin in a small bowl. Adjust salt and lime to taste, if needed.

MAKE THE PIZZA: In a small bowl mix the cream cheese with the thecha chutney.

Heat a large skillet or a griddle over medium-high heat. Spread a thin layer of butter on both sides of the naan, and working in batches if necessary, cook in the skillet until golden, about 2 minutes per side. Keep the naan warm in the preheated oven while you fry the eggs (see the Pro Tip on page 32).

Place the warm toasted naan on a serving plate and spread with one-fourth of the chutney and cream cheese mixture. Top with half of a sliced avocado, a sprinkle of salt and pepper, and two fried eggs. Add a generous spoonful of the salsa and serve with a lime wedge. Repeat with the remaining ingredients to make four naan pizzas in all. Eat immediately!

TURKISH EGGS

Serves 4

For the cilantro and parsley oil

- ¼ cup (10 g) finely chopped fresh cilantro
- ¼ cup (13 g) finely chopped fresh parsley
- 2 serrano chiles, finely chopped
- 2 teaspoons minced garlic
- 1 teaspoon ground coriander
- 1 teaspoon ground cumin
- 1 teaspoon red chili powder
- ½ teaspoon salt
- ⅓ cup (75 ml) extra-virgin olive oil

For the eggs

- 2 cups (480 ml) full-fat plain Greek yogurt, at room temperature
- 4 cloves garlic, grated
- ½ teaspoon salt
- 8 fried eggs (see Pro Tip, page 32)
- 1 teaspoon za'atar
- 2 tablespoons finely chopped fresh dill
- Warm naan or pita, for serving

PRO TIP

Grating the garlic on a Microplane gives it more of a kick and a uniform texture.

My husband, Pinank, and I were lucky enough to visit Istanbul in 2015, and it remains one of our favorite trips to date. We would stroll Istiklal Street every day, stopping at stalls for kebabs, finishing every meal with mint tea. For breakfast each morning, we'd have cilbir, better known as Turkish eggs! Years later, when I saw recipes for this dish going viral on the internet, I was inspired to make my own version. It includes a spicy green cilantro and parsley oil that adds earthy depth to the tart and creamy Greek yogurt in this dish. I always double the recipe for this garlicky green sauce because it tastes great whipped into Greek yogurt for a simple dip, on meats, or drizzled over a plain fried egg in the morning. While only a small amount of za'atar is called for in this recipe, it drops a flavor bomb on this dish, so it's worth keeping some of this herby Middle Eastern spice on hand. Also, if you want to add a little heat here, some red pepper flakes, hot pepper, or Aleppo pepper will make these eggs really pop!

MAKE THE CILANTRO AND PARSLEY OIL: In a small bowl, mix together the cilantro, parsley, serranos, garlic, coriander, cumin, chili powder, and salt. In a small saucepan set over low heat, gently warm the oil, taking care not to let it overheat. Immediately pour the oil mixture over the herbs and set aside.

MAKE THE BASE FOR THE EGGS: In a small bowl, thoroughly mix the yogurt, garlic, and salt. Divide and spread the mixture equally on the bottom of four plates.

Place 2 eggs on top of the yogurt on each plate. Drizzle each serving with the cilantro and parsley oil and sprinkle with the za'atar and dill. Serve immediately with warm flatbread.

ZUCCHINI DANGELA

Serves 6

1 cup (180 g) basmati rice

½ cup (100 g) chana dal

½ cup (95 g) toor dal

1½ cups (135 g) peeled and shredded zucchini (from about 5 ounces zucchini)

2 tablespoon minced garlic

2 tablespoons peeled and minced fresh ginger

3 tablespoons minced serrano chiles

⅓ cup (75 ml) whole-milk plain yogurt

½ teaspoon ground turmeric

2 tablespoons grated jaggery or granulated sugar

2 teaspoons ajwain seeds, crushed between your fingertips

¼ cup (10 g) finely chopped fresh cilantro

2¼ teaspoons salt

2 tablespoons canola or vegetable oil, plus more for the griddle

1 teaspoon brown mustard seeds

¼ teaspoon hing (asafetida)

Sesame seeds

1 cup (240 ml) full-fat plain yogurt

2 tablespoons Cilantro Chutney (page 193)

This breakfast and brunch dish, made popular in western India, is a staple in Gujarati homes. Similar to a savory crepe, dangela are made with shredded bottle gourd, but I swapped it here for zucchini. The batter, made from soaked rice and lentils, is traditionally used to make handvo, which is a baked, dense, savory cake-like dish. However, its counterpart, dangela, are thinner and are made in a skillet, allowing for a more delicious, crispy crust on top. I ate a ton of these when I was postpartum because the batter freezes extremely well, and it was so convenient to grab from the freezer and have something hot and hearty to enjoy during those crazy-busy mornings. I will warn you that this recipe can be a bit of work, so you definitely want to plan ahead. The rice and lentils need to soak for 4 to 6 hours, and quite a bit of garlic, ginger, and green chiles need to be blended with a high-speed blender, which can be done the day before to save time. My favorite part of a dangela is the addition of toasty sesame seeds sprinkled on each one as it cooks, because it adds a little nutty flavor and wonderful texture. I add a dollop of yogurt to my Cilantro Chutney to use as a quick dipping sauce, and I love these with masala chai for a brunch, or with a cold glass of milk, eaten right out of the pan!

Place the rice, chana dal, and toor dal in a fine-mesh colander and rinse 3 to 4 times until the water runs clear. Place the mixture in a large bowl, cover with fresh cool water, and set aside to soak for 4 to 6 hours. Drain the water and transfer the mixture to a high-speed blender.

Add 1 cup (240 ml) water to the blender. Mix well, scraping down the sides of the blender as needed, until partially smooth, but with some grit remaining in the texture.

Transfer the batter to a large bowl and add the zucchini, garlic, ginger, serranos, yogurt, turmeric, jaggery, ajwain, cilantro, salt, and 1 tablespoon of the oil. Mix well to combine.

Meanwhile, in a very small pot, heat the remaining 1 tablespoon oil over medium heat. When the oil is hot, add the mustard seeds carefully as the oil may splatter. Once the mustard seeds begin to pop, 5 to 10 seconds, quickly remove them from the heat, add the hing, and carefully stir to release its fragrance. Gently mix the spice-infused oil into the batter. The batter should have the consistency of pancake batter; add additional water if necessary to thin it.

Heat a large cast-iron skillet or griddle over medium-high heat. Lightly coat the pan or griddle with canola oil. Ladle about ¼ cup (60 ml) of the batter into the center of the griddle, and using the back of the ladle or a spoon, spread the batter out into one thin, even layer to create an

approximately 6-inch (15 cm) disc. Sprinkle about ½ teaspoon sesame seeds over the top and, once the bottom is golden brown, about 2 minutes, flip and continue to cook for 2 additional minutes until the second side is golden brown. Transfer to a platter and continue cooking the remaining batter, adding additional oil between pancakes, as needed. You should have about 16 pancakes in all. Mix the yogurt into the chutney and serve in small bowls alongside the pancakes.

Mini
CURRIED EGG SALAD
SANDWICHES

Makes 8 mini sandwiches

1   cup (240 ml) mayonnaise

3   cloves garlic, grated

1½   teaspoons curry powder

½   teaspoon cayenne pepper

½   teaspoon garam masala

¼   teaspoon salt

¼   cup (10 g) finely chopped fresh cilantro

1   jalapeño or serrano chile, finely diced (optional)

1   small stalk celery, finely diced

6   hard-boiled eggs, peeled and chopped

8   mini croissants, sliced in half horizontally

Adding a bit of curry powder and other Indian spices takes typical egg salad from dull to delish! I love serving this chunky salad inside mini croissants for brunch, or on a rustic piece of sourdough bread for lunch. It's also great with crackers for a satisfying snack.

In a large bowl, mix together the mayonnaise, garlic, curry powder, cayenne, garam masala, salt, cilantro, jalapeño (if using), and celery. Add the chopped eggs and use a silicone spatula to gently mix until combined. Refrigerate if you are not serving right away. Place a few tablespoons of the egg salad in each mini croissant and serve.

ASPARAGUS & PEPPER JACK ROSTI

with TARRAGON-GARLIC AIOLI

Serves 6

1 (16-ounce/455 g) bag plain unseasoned frozen hash browns (or if seasoned, omit the salt below)

4 ounces (115 g) pepper Jack cheese, shredded (about 1 cup)

¼ teaspoon ground turmeric

¼ cup (13 g) finely chopped fresh parsley

Freshly ground black pepper

¾ teaspoon salt

3 tablespoons ghee or clarified butter

½ teaspoon mustard seeds

½ teaspoon cumin seeds

1 serrano chile, finely chopped

8 to 10 curry leaves

Small pinch hing (asafetida)

2 bunches asparagus, trimmed and sliced crosswise into ¼-inch (6 mm) pieces (2 heaping cups/280 g)

1 recipe Tarragon Aioli (page 256)

Okay, I know this recipe is supposed to be about the rosti, and we will get there, but I'd be doing you all a huge disservice if I didn't start by singing the praises of the Tarragon Aioli first. In true condiment-obsessed fashion, I spent a solid week sending all my friends a screenshot of this aioli recipe with "YOU NEED TO MAKE THIS" in overly aggressive caps followed by at least four exclamation points. It's packed with one of my favorite herbs—tarragon—and even though it's got a mayo base, it still feels light and bright, so I make it weekly to dip into with just about anything. Now back to the rosti, which, if you're unfamiliar with it, is a Swiss potato pancake made with roasted or boiled potatoes. I made this version using frozen hash browns to save time, and of course my spin on it involves adding a tadka (infused oil) of curry leaves and warm spices. The outside is super crisp and the inside is soft and fluffy—it reminds me of diner hash browns, but elevated. The Tarragon Aioli balances the rich heartiness of the rosti and adds a level of sophistication that is sure to impress at brunch!

In a large bowl, crumble the hash browns with your hands—they should be almost fluffy, not frozen clumps (you want them to be cold, so only remove them from the freezer once you've done most of the prep). Add the shredded cheese, turmeric, parsley, a few grinds of pepper, and ½ teaspoon of the salt, and toss to combine.

In a 10-inch (25 cm) nonstick pan set over medium-high heat, melt 1 tablespoon of the ghee. Add the mustard seeds, and when they begin to splutter, in 10 to 15 seconds, stir in the cumin seeds, serrano, curry leaves, and hing. Add the asparagus and remaining ¼ teaspoon salt and cook for 2 to 3 minutes, until the asparagus is lightly golden brown and crisp-tender. Transfer the asparagus to the potato mixture and gently stir to combine.

continues

PRO TIPS

You can make the batter ahead of time, freeze it for up to 6 weeks, and fry the rosti on the day you plan to serve them. To trim the asparagus, snap off and discard the overly fibrous bottoms by holding the stalk at both ends and snapping until the tough bottom breaks off.

Return the pan to medium-high heat and add 1 tablespoon of the ghee to the pan. When the ghee is sizzling, add the potato mixture to the pan, and using a spatula, press the mixture evenly to form a pancake. Cook the mixture for 10 to 12 minutes, lowering the heat as needed so the potatoes cook evenly and form a crisp crust on the underside. Using a heatproof spatula, occasionally push the sides of the pancake away from the edges and gently lift the bottom to check for even browning, and turn the pan around over the heat source to also encourage the pancake to brown evenly.

Carefully remove the pan from the heat and place a large heatproof plate (or large flat cookie sheet, if you don't have a big enough plate) over the pan and flip the potato pancake onto the plate. (I suggest using oven mitts to do this.) Add the remaining tablespoon of ghee to the pan and simply slide the pancake back in the pan, crispy side up, and continue cooking about 4 minutes, until the bottom is slightly crisp.

Carefully slide the rosti onto a platter and serve with the tarragon aioli on the side, or dollop the aioli on top of the rosti before serving.

Banana–Cardamom
CRUMB MUFFINS

Makes 1 dozen muffins

1½ cups (190 g) all-purpose flour

1 teaspoon baking powder

1 teaspoon baking soda

1 teaspoon ground cardamom

½ teaspoon ground cinnamon

¼ teaspoon ground nutmeg

½ teaspoon salt

3 ripe bananas, mashed (about 1¼ cups)

½ cup (100 g) granulated sugar

⅓ cup packed (75 g) brown sugar

1 tablespoon vanilla extract

1 large egg, lightly beaten

⅓ cup (75 ml) canola oil

For the crumb topping

⅔ cup (80 g) all-purpose flour

5 tablespoons packed (70 g) brown sugar

¼ teaspoon ground cardamom

¼ teaspoon ground cinnamon

4 tablespoons (55 g) unsalted butter, melted

PRO TIP

When testing baked goods for doneness with a toothpick or knife, test in a couple of different spots, as you may hit a wet chunk of fruit and mistake that for an underdone treat.

The combination of cardamom (the quintessential spice found in almost every Indian dessert) with cinnamon and brown sugar makes this my hands-down favorite muffin. It tastes like a cross between banana bread and a coffee cake, and the crumbly topping totally sends it over the top! My favorite way to enjoy these is right out of the oven, with an ice-cold glass of milk. And while I am fully aware that these are in the breakfast chapter, you can enjoy them any time of day! I've even served them for dessert: Split them in half, toast them in a skillet with some butter, and top with a little vanilla ice cream and caramel for a bananas Foster vibe.

Grease or line 12 muffin tins with paper cups. Preheat the oven to 375°F (190°C).

In a medium bowl, whisk together the flour, baking powder, baking soda, cardamom, cinnamon, nutmeg, and salt.

In a large bowl, mix the mashed bananas, both sugars, the vanilla extract, egg, and oil until well combined. Gently stir the dry ingredients into the banana mixture, taking care not to overmix or the muffins will be tough and rubbery.

MAKE THE CRUMB TOPPING: Combine the flour, brown sugar, cardamom, cinnamon, and butter in a bowl. Gently rub the dry ingredients with the butter between your fingertips until you have pea-size crumbs.

Fill the muffin tin cups with the banana mixture until they are approximately two-thirds full. Top each muffin tin evenly with the crumb mixture and bake in the preheated oven for 18 to 22 minutes, or until a toothpick inserted in the center of a muffin comes out clean. Let cool in the pan for 10 minutes on a rack before serving. Carefully run a knife or small offset spatula around the rim of each muffin and gently pop them out of the tin.

BANANA–CARDAMOM CRUMB
MUFFINS, PAGE 45

CORNFLAKES CHEVDO

Makes 8 cups

4 tablespoons (60 g) canola or vegetable oil

½ cup (70 g) raw peanuts

2 teaspoons mustard seeds

3 teaspoons sesame seeds

⅛ teaspoon hing (aseftida)

15 curry leaves

¼ teaspoon ground turmeric

1 (12-ounce/340 g) box cornflakes

½ teaspoon salt

2½ teaspoons red chili powder

1 tablespoon confectioners' sugar

Spicy, savory, and a little bit sweet, this Gujarati snack mix is a staple in our house. I enjoy it with a hot cup of chai in the morning, or as a little afternoon snack to hold me over until dinnertime.

Heat the oil in a large pot or wok over medium-high heat. Add the peanuts and cook until they start to get a bit of color, about 1 minute. Add the mustard seeds and let them sizzle for a few seconds, then add the sesame seeds, hing, curry leaves, and turmeric. Reduce the heat to low, add the entire box of cornflakes, and mix well, stirring gently. Add the salt and chili powder and cook for 4 to 5 minutes, until the cereal is golden in color and crisp. Add the confectioners' sugar and remove from the heat.

Let cool completely and then transfer to an airtight container to store for up to 1 week.

Overnight
MANGO CHIA PUDDING

Serves 4

1 cup (165 g) chia seeds

2 tablespoons packed brown sugar or honey

3 cups (600 ml) almond milk or coconut-almond milk

1 teaspoon vanilla extract

1 teaspoon ground cardamon

1 teaspoon ground cinnamon

2 tablespoons orange blossom water

Toppings

2 mangos, peeled and diced

¾ cup (70 g) sliced almonds

⅓ cup (30 g) coconut chips or shredded sweetened coconut flakes

1 tablespoon honey

PRO TIP

Portion this pudding into individual servings in glass jars in the fridge so you can pop one out for breakfast or for a quick snack. Or, if you're serving this to a crowd, it would be gorgeous arranged in a trifle!

Breakfast that you don't have to wake up and make is the best kind of breakfast, am I right?! This overnight chia pudding is an effortless option for busy weekdays, but I love that it's also elegant enough to serve for a weekend brunch. While I'm a big fan of the combination of mango and coconut in the topping, feel free to add or swap out ingredients based on what you have on hand, or what's in season. You can top this off with any sort of berries, or dried fruit such as apricots would be a flavorful choice (strawberries and mini chocolate chips are delish, too!). Chia seeds are relatively mild in flavor and widely known for being a source of fiber, but if you want to up the nutrition even more, add a spoonful of nut butter to the pudding mixture.

In a large bowl, combine the chia seeds, brown sugar, almond milk, vanilla, cardamom, cinnamon, and orange blossom water. Stir until very well combined and the pudding is starting to thicken. Eat immediately or refrigerate for up to 48 hours for a thicker pudding.

Top the pudding with mango, almonds, and coconut, and drizzle with honey.

SUNRISE CITRUS SMOOTHIE

Serves 4

- 4 heaping cups (about 700 g) fresh or frozen pineapple
- 2 tablespoons lemon juice
- 4 tangerines, peeled and separated into wedges
- 1 cup (240 ml) almond milk or milk of choice
- 20 fresh mint leaves
- 4 mint sprigs for garnish

When I was pregnant with Sahil, I had a major craving for all things refreshing and citrusy. Popsicles, ice-cold oranges, and lots and lots of pineapple. Had. To. Have. It! This smoothie, which is more like a slushy, doesn't have yogurt or a lot of milk, so the bright, sweet, and tart flavor of the tangerines and the pineapple really shines through. Plus, the small handful of mint in this drink also brings about those *Wait, what is that?* looks every time I've served it. This is ideal in the warmer months due to its refreshing nature, but if you can't get fresh pineapple, you can swap in frozen or canned. To make this heartier, add a big scoop of Greek yogurt, more milk, and/or a handful of greens such as spinach or kale. It's also wonderful blended with a tiny piece of ginger or turmeric root for added zing.

If you're using fresh pineapple, place a handful of ice in the blender first; add the pineapple, lemon juice, tangerines, milk, and mint leaves and blend until smooth. If you're using frozen pineapple, place the pineapple in the blender first, then add the lemon juice, tangerines, milk, and mint leaves and blend until smooth. Garnish with the reserved mint sprigs and serve chilled.

TAHINI, COFFEE & CHIKOO *SHAKE*

Serves 4

3 tablespoons sugar

8 ounces (240 ml) hot brewed coffee

12 ounces (340 g) frozen chikoo, defrosted for 15 minutes

1 tablespoon vanilla extract

1½ cups (360 ml) milk of your choice (I use 2% milk)

½ teaspoon ground cardamom

2 teaspoons unsweetened cocoa powder

¼ cup (60 ml) tahini

Ice, for serving

PRO TIP

There are a few steps you need to do ahead: Make sure the coffee is warm enough to dissolve the sugar, but not piping hot, because it needs to be cool before you make the shake. You'll need to defrost the chikoo for 15 minutes while you get everything else together.

If you're ever in Philly, you've got to hit up Goldie, a famous Israeli falafel shop with multiple locations in the city, for their most delicious tehina shakes! They're decadent, nutty, and after having them many times, I slowly found myself adding a bit of tahini to many of my own shakes. My favorite by far has been the combination of chikoo + tahini + coffee. Chikoo, a fruit native to India, might be difficult to find in the United States in its fresh form, but frozen chikoo is readily available at South Asian markets and works great with this smoothie. To lighten these up, you can swap the sugar for some soaked dates and swap the tahini for almond butter, or even throw in a scoop of oats for additional nutrition. If you want to make this as a dessert, a scoop of coffee ice cream would give it a rich, velvety texture.

Dissolve the sugar in the hot coffee and chill.

In a blender, combine the sweetened coffee, the chikoo, vanilla, milk, cardamom, cocoa powder, and tahini and blend until smooth. Serve over ice.

SOUPS

Whenever I check in with my *Chutney Life* readers and ask them what new recipes they're looking for, it's no surprise that "easy and convenient" are always at the top of their lists, quickly followed by "flavorful and nutritious." I'm happy to report that the hearty soups in this chapter check all those boxes. And even better news, these one-pot meals equal less stress, and less mess during preparation.

These recipes are all about taking advantage of what's in your pantry. If you're like me, you probably have TONS of beans, chiles, noodles, spices, broth, coconut milk, and more at the ready. Add a few fresh herbs and veggies and you're good to go! These soups are filling enough to be a meal on their own, or can be rounded out with your favorite bread, naan, or crackers and a salad.

The advance prep that soup allows for is the perfect way to relieve mealtime stress. You can make a batch to last you through the week (serve it for dinner one night and reheat it for a tasty, quick lunch later in the week), or you can double down and make two batches at once, freezing one to heat up later on, when you're running short on time and need to put dinner together superfast!

That said, these soups aren't *just* for quick and easy meals. They are also ideal for rounding out a menu. When I'm entertaining and I feel like I need one more thing and don't want to have to deal with the oven, soup is my go-to. As an elegant first course for a Saturday night dinner party, or served straight out of the Crock-Pot after some fall or winter outdoor fun, soup nails it.

Here you'll find a range of bowl-filling goodness, featuring my favorites, as well as my take on classics, such as Chana Masala Minestrone (page 63), where traditional Italian flavors combine with Indian spices; zuppa Toscana (page 64), a vegetarian version with hearty lentils taking the place of sausage; Miso Noodle Soup (page 71), which is the perfect healing vegetarian swap for chicken noodle soup, guaranteed to settle your stomach and open your sinuses; and Upgraded Campbell's Tomato Soup with Chile Cheese Croutons (page 67) brings coming inside for tomato soup and grilled cheese as a kid to a whole new level. Whatever the season or occasion, this chapter has the soup covered!

COCONUT CURRY *NOODLE* SOUP

Serves 4

1 (10-ounce/280 g) package ramen noodles

1 tablespoon unrefined/virgin coconut oil

1 (13½-ounce/405 ml) can full-fat coconut milk, cream and water separated (do not shake can before opening)

2 tablespoons plus 1 teaspoon panang curry paste

2 teaspoons grated garlic

2 teaspoons grated fresh ginger

½ medium onion, thinly sliced

½ red bell pepper, thinly sliced

5 ounces (140 g) sliced shiitake mushrooms

½ teaspoon salt, plus more as needed

4 cups (about 1 L) vegetable broth

2 tablespoons soy sauce

2 tablespoons fish sauce

1½ tablespoons fresh lime juice

2 tablespoons packed brown sugar, plus more as needed

1½ teaspoons gochugaru (Korean chili powder) or crushed red pepper, plus more if you like it spicy

2 tablespoons chopped fresh cilantro

Lime wedges, for garnish

There is nothing more comforting than a big bowl of soupy, spicy noodles. This soup is a bit heavier on the noodle to broth ratio than your typical noodle soup, because every time I make it with more broth, everyone asks if there are more noodles! Moral of the story: There is *no* such thing as too many noodles. I particularly love Thai food for the way it perfectly balances sweet, salty, and spicy flavors. I recommend you use the quantities below as a starting point and adjust the sugar, soy sauce, lime, and gochugaru based on your own preferences—and how much heat you can handle! I'm also totally not above begging you to take a trip to your local Asian market to buy fresh ramen noodles for their delicious chewy texture (freeze any extras) and panang curry paste (I love the brand Maesri, which can also be found on Amazon). If you're not serving the soup right away, keep the noodles and broth separate to prevent the noodles from getting mushy. Add shredded chicken or thinly sliced beef, pork, or tofu to make this soup an even heartier meal.

Bring a pot of water to a boil and cook the ramen noodles according to package directions. Drain and reserve.

In a dutch oven or large heavy-bottomed pot, melt the coconut oil over medium heat. Add the reserved coconut cream, the curry paste, garlic, and ginger. Cook for 1 to 2 minutes, stirring constantly, until the garlic and ginger are fragrant. Add the onion, peppers, mushrooms, and salt and cook until they begin to soften, 3 to 5 minutes. Stir in the broth and the coconut water from the can, cover the pot, reduce the heat to medium-low, and let simmer for 10 minutes.

Remove the lid and stir in the soy sauce, fish sauce, lime juice, and brown sugar and simmer for 2 minutes. Add the gochugaru and the cooked noodles. Taste for sweetness, spice, and salt and adjust as needed. Serve in bowls topped with chopped cilantro and lime wedges.

Chana Masala
MINESTRONE

Serves 4

- 4 ounces (115 g) uncooked ditalini pasta
- 2 tablespoons canola or vegetable oil
- 1 teaspoon cumin seeds
- ¼ teaspoon hing (asafetida)
- 1 (½-inch/12 mm) piece cinnamon stick
- 2 cloves
- 2 bay leaves
- 2 star anise
- 1 medium onion, diced
- 1 large carrot, diced
- 1 large stalk celery, diced
- ¾ teaspoon salt, plus more if needed
- 1 tablespoon minced garlic
- ½ teaspoon peeled and minced fresh ginger
- 2 tablespoons tomato paste
- ½ teaspoon Italian seasoning
- 1 teaspoon red chili powder
- 1 teaspoon ground coriander
- ½ teaspoon ground turmeric
- 1 teaspoon garam masala
- 4 cups (about 1 L) vegetable broth
- 1 cup (110 g) green beans cut into ½-inch (12 mm) pieces
- 1 (15.5-ounce/439 g) can chickpeas, drained and rinsed
- ¼ cup (25 g) freshly grated Parmesan cheese, plus more for serving
- 1 tablespoon finely chopped fresh parsley
- 1 tablespoon finely chopped fresh cilantro

I'll be honest, this recipe took multiple tries to get just right. In my mind I had conjured up the idea of a minestrone soup that was hearty but light, and with the perfect blend of Indian and Italian flavors. After making many versions, I found that adding whole spices was crucial to give the broth depth and carry the flavors through every spoonful. The aromatics are reminiscent of a delicious chana masala (also known as chole), but packed with vegetables instead of just chickpeas. This recipe calls for a bit of chopping in the vegetable department, so if you're trying to make this soup faster, toss in a bag of frozen mixed vegetables as an easy-but-still-totally-counts-as-effort sort of swap for the fresh veggies!

Cook the ditalini pasta according to package directions. Drain and set aside.

In a dutch oven or large heavy-bottomed pot, heat the oil over medium-high heat. Add the cumin seeds and the hing and let the seeds splutter for a few seconds. Add the cinnamon stick, cloves, bay leaves, and star anise and stir until the spices are fragrant, 20 to 30 seconds.

Reduce the heat to medium, add the onion, carrot, celery, and salt and cook for about 10 minutes, stirring occasionally, until the onions are golden. Add the garlic, ginger, and tomato paste and cook for an additional 2 to 3 minutes, until the garlic is fragrant. Add the Italian seasoning, chili powder, coriander, turmeric, and garam masala. Stir and cook for 2 to 3 minutes. Pour in the broth and add the green beans. Increase the heat to bring the mixture to a boil, then cover the pot and reduce the heat to a simmer and cook for 10 minutes. Remove the lid, add the chickpeas, replace the lid, and simmer for an additional 10 minutes.

Carefully remove the cinnamon stick, cloves, star anise, and bay leaves and discard. Stir in the cheese, parsley, cilantro, and cooked pasta. Remove from the heat, taste and adjust the salt, ladle into bowls, and top with more grated cheese.

Soup can be stored in an airtight container in the fridge for up to 5 days or frozen for up to 3 months.

PRO TIP

Add the ditalini at the very end and cook it completely (not al dente), as it will soak up more of the liquid the more uncooked it is and the longer it sits in the broth. Serve this hearty soup with crusty garlic bread for dipping.

Vegetarian ZUPPA TOSCANA

with LENTILS

Serves 4 to 6

6 ounces (170 g) uncooked brown or green lentils, rinsed and drained

1 bay leaf

Salt

2 tablespoons extra-virgin olive oil

2 yellow onions, diced

1 tablespoon minced garlic

1 medium russet potato, peeled and diced

1½ teaspoons ground fennel

1½ teaspoons Cajun seasoning

1 teaspoon Italian seasoning

½ teaspoon crushed red pepper

6 cups (180 ml) vegetable broth

1 bunch (200 g) Tuscan kale, center ribs removed and leaves cut into ½-inch (12 mm) pieces

¾ cup (180 ml) heavy cream

2 teaspoons fresh lemon juice

2 tablespoons finely chopped fresh parsley

⅔ cup (70 g) freshly grated Pecorino Romano

While traditional zuppa Toscana is made with sausage, kale, and potatoes, this vegetarian version that calls for lentils remains as hearty as the original—so trust me, you totally won't miss the meat. This soup has a rich, buttery finish, and the first time I gave someone a taste, they likened it to what fettuccine Alfredo would taste like if you could drink it . . . so again, *definitely rich*. While it's creamy, this soup is not thick like a bisque, so you can enjoy it year-round. I also find it to be off the beaten path enough to serve as an impressive first course at a dinner party! If you want to up the veggies in here, toss in a handful of chopped zucchini and mushrooms with the onions. To make it dairy-free, swap the cream for coconut milk and omit the Pecorino.

In a medium pot, add the lentils, 8 cups (2 L) water, and the bay leaf. Bring to a boil, add a pinch of salt, reduce the heat, and simmer for 20 to 30 minutes, until the lentils are just cooked through. (They will continue to cook in the soup, so they should not be too firm, but they should not be mushy either.) Drain and set aside.

Meanwhile, in a dutch oven or large heavy-bottomed pot, heat the oil over medium heat. Add the onions and cook until they are golden around the edges, about 5 minutes, stirring occasionally.

Next, add the garlic, potato, fennel, Cajun seasoning, Italian seasoning, and the crushed red pepper. Stir until the garlic is fragrant, for about 30 seconds. Add the broth and bring to a boil. Cover, reduce the heat to medium-low, and cook for 10 minutes, until the potatoes are fork-tender.

Add the cooked lentils, kale, cream, and lemon juice and stir well to combine. Reduce the heat to low and simmer for 5 minutes to bring the flavors together. Turn off the heat, add the parsley and Pecorino Romano, and taste to adjust for salt. Serve immediately.

Upgraded CAMPBELL'S TOMATO SOUP

with CHILE CHEESE CROUTONS

Serves 4

- 1 tablespoon canola or vegetable oil
- 1 tablespoon minced garlic
- 2 teaspoons peeled and minced fresh ginger
- 2 tablespoons store-bought chile garlic sauce
- 1 teaspoon ground cumin
- ½ teaspoon ground coriander
- ½ teaspoon red chili powder
- 1 tablespoon ketchup
- 2 tablespoons soy sauce
- 2 heaping tablespoons finely chopped fresh cilantro
- 1 (23.2-ounce/685 ml) can or 2 (10½-ounce/310 ml) cans Campbell's Tomato Soup

For the chile cheese croutons

- 4 tablespoons (60 ml) Cilantro Chutney (page 193)
- 8 slices sandwich bread
- ½ cup (120 ml) mayonnaise, plus more as needed
- 4 ounces (115 g) shredded Monterey Jack cheese (about 1 cup)
- 4 tablespoons (½ stick/55 g) unsalted butter

I've grown up loving a bowl of classic tomato soup, sometimes even a bisque, but the first time I had tomato soup on a trip to India I knew there was no going back. It was anything but basic: It had notes of garlic, ginger, and a tangy sweetness I couldn't quite put my finger on. Since then, I've ordered tomato soup at every Indian restaurant where I see it on the menu, in both India and in the United States. This recipe is reminiscent of the versions I've enjoyed over the years, and because I rarely have fresh tomatoes just sitting in the fridge, it's made by doctoring up a can of good ole Campbell's Tomato Soup. To take it up another notch, I top it off with croutons made from grilled cheese sandwiches that have Cilantro Chutney in them. But if you want to make the classic lunch, you can leave the grilled cheese whole and dunk each bite into the soup.

In a large heavy-bottomed pot, heat the oil over medium heat, add the garlic and ginger, and cook until fragrant, 30 seconds to 1 minute, stirring frequently. Add the chile garlic sauce, cumin, coriander, chili powder, ketchup, soy sauce, and cilantro and cook for 2 to 3 minutes, stirring so the spices won't burn. Pour in the soup, and then fill the empty can (or cans) with the equivalent amount of water and add it to the pot. Bring to a boil, cover, then reduce to the heat to low and simmer for 8 minutes.

MEANWHILE, PREPARE THE CHILE CHEESE CROUTONS: Spread 1 tablespoon of the cilantro chutney on one slice of bread and spread 1 tablespoon of the mayonnaise on another slice of bread. Sprinkle one-quarter of the cheese on top of the chutney and close the sandwich. For a beautiful golden crust, spread a thin layer of mayo on the outside of both sides of the sandwich. Repeat the process for the remaining 3 sandwiches.

Working in batches, melt 1 tablespoon butter in a wide skillet set over medium-high heat and cook the sandwich until the cheese is melted and the bread is evenly browned on both sides, 2 to 3 minutes. In between batches, wipe the pan. Remove the crusts from the bread and cut the sandwiches into crouton-size cubes.

To serve, ladle the soup into individual bowls and divide the croutons evenly among the bowls.

Too Good to Be True
CORN SOUP

Serves 4

4 teaspoons unsalted butter

3 shallots, finely chopped

2 cloves garlic, peeled

Salt

1 teaspoon ground coriander

Pinch cayenne pepper

4 cups (540 g) frozen sweet yellow corn, thawed (or use fresh corn kernels cut from the cob; see Pro Tip)

4 cups (about 1 L) vegetable broth or water

Freshly ground black pepper

2 tablespoons finely chopped chives, for garnish

PRO TIP

If you're using fresh corn, simmer the cobs in the broth for 15 minutes to amp up the corn flavor.

This may quite honestly be the simplest recipe in this cookbook. As you skim through the ingredients, you might even find yourself wondering if it's worth a try, because at first glance, the recipe really does sound too good to be true. Trust me, I feel you, but when I say this recipe delivers on flavor, I mean it. Sweet summer corn, whether you're using fresh or frozen, gets cooked with butter and coriander until it's soft and tender. Then, blend it to get an ultra-creamy consistency that would make someone assume there was a generous amount of cream hiding in it, but there's no milk or cream to be found. If you want to make this vegan, simply replace the butter with vegan butter. This recipe is also a perfect example of when it's worth it to toast and grind your own spices, as the flavor from freshly ground coriander seeds will become even more aromatic and pronounced. Enjoy this as a simple lunch on its own, or serve it with the Veggie Hummus Sandwich (page 113), the Chopped Kuchumba Salad with Spiced Sourdough Croutons (page 83), or other salad or sandwich of your choice.

Melt the butter in a dutch oven or heavy-bottomed pot over medium-high heat. Add the shallots, garlic, and ½ teaspoon salt, and cook until the shallots are translucent, 5 to 7 minutes. Add the coriander and stir for about 30 seconds, until fragrant. Add the cayenne, corn kernels, broth, and 1 teaspoon salt (or as needed, depending on the saltiness of the broth) and simmer for about 10 minutes, until the corn is cooked through but still slightly firm.

Working in batches, carefully transfer all but 1 cup (240 ml) of the soup to a blender, and blend until completely smooth, taking care not to overfill the blender or the hot soup will spill over the sides during blending. (If you want a completely smooth texture, blend all of the soup in batches.) Return the blended soup and the 1 cup (240 ml) unblended soup to the pot, season with freshly ground black pepper, and adjust salt to taste. Ladle into soup bowls, garnish with the chives, and serve.

MISO NOODLE SOUP

Serves 4

2 (10-ounce/225 g) packages ramen noodles

2 teaspoons unrefined/virgin coconut oil

1 serrano chile, finely chopped, plus more for finishing (optional)

3 green onions, finely sliced (dark green parts separated)

2 carrots, peeled, halved lengthwise and cut into half-moons

3 teaspoons salt, plus more if needed

1 teaspoon minced garlic

1 (1-inch/2.5 cm) piece fresh ginger, peeled and grated

2½ tablespoons sweet white miso paste

1 tablespoon lemon juice

¼ cup (10 g) finely chopped fresh cilantro, plus more for serving

Lemon wedges, for serving

You know when you're just not feeling well, and you need one of those soups that's going to embrace you with a warm hug from the inside out? The kind of soup that clears out your sinuses? Well, this Miso Noodle Soup is it. Like classic chicken noodle soup, this comforting, rich broth restores you from the inside out with each and every sip. The white miso paste adds depth and flavor in a similar way that a long-simmered chicken or vegetable stock does, but with WAY less effort. I like to add the noodles to each bowl right before serving so they don't soak up too much of the broth, but if you want to just simply sip on this soup in one of those giant bowl mugs, then skip the noodles and it will still be delicious. The coconut oil rounds out the sweetness here, but you can swap in a neutral oil or toasted sesame oil for a more distinct flavor. I've used ramen noodles here but feel free to try egg noodles to mimic a chicken soup, or rice noodles, soba noodles, or even a scoop of rice. For extra sinus clearing, garnish with a few fresh slices of serrano chiles.

Prepare the noodles according to package directions. Drain and set aside.

Meanwhile, in a dutch oven or large heavy-bottomed pot, heat the coconut oil over medium-high heat, add the serrano, and stir for a few seconds. Add the white and pale green parts of the green onions, the carrots, and salt and cook, stirring frequently, until the green onions and carrots have softened, 2 to 3 minutes. Add the garlic and ginger and reduce the heat to medium, stirring frequently for about 1 minute until fragrant, taking care not to burn the aromatics.

Add 6 cups (1.4 L) water, raise the heat to bring the mixture to a boil, then reduce the heat to a simmer. Remove 1 cup (240 ml) of the soup to a small bowl and whisk the miso paste into it until the miso is completely incorporated. (If you add it directly to the soup you may find lumps of miso later!) Add the miso mixture to the soup and simmer for 2 minutes.

Turn off the heat and gently stir in the lemon juice, cilantro, dark green parts of the green scallions, and the noodles. Adjust salt to taste. Garnish with lemon wedges, more fresh cilantro, and additional green chiles, if you like.

Fiery
PINTO BEAN SOUP

Serves 4 to 6

2 tablespoons canola oil

1 teaspoon cumin seeds

2 serrano chiles, finely chopped

2 green onions, finely sliced (dark green parts separated), plus more for garnish (optional)

2½ cups (315 g) finely chopped onions (from 1 to 2 large onions)

1 teaspoon salt, plus more if needed

1 tablespoon canned tomato paste

2 teaspoons taco seasoning

½ teaspoon dried oregano, preferably Mexican oregano

1 teaspoon ground coriander

1 tablespoon minced garlic

1 (14½-ounce/415 g) can diced tomatoes with green chiles

½ cup (20 g) finely chopped fresh cilantro

1 (4½-ounce/130 g) can diced green chiles

1 tablespoon adobo from canned chipotles in adobo

1 (15-ounce/430 g) can pinto beans, rinsed and drained

4 cups (about 1 L) vegetable or chicken broth

Optional garnishes

Avocado, cilantro, shredded cheese (Monterey Jack or cheddar), tortilla strips, pico de gallo, sour cream

I first shared this recipe on my blog during the height of the pandemic, when everyone was cooped up inside and wanted easy, pantry-friendly meals that still delivered on flavor. It quickly became a *Chutney Life* fan favorite, so I had to include it in this chapter because it's both a crowd-pleaser and a satisfying weeknight meal. With its high-octane heat, this hearty soup is perfect during cold-weather months, and while I'm a fan of pinto beans for their texture, you can try it with most any kind of bean. Moreover, with an array of fresh toppings, this soup won't feel like you tossed together a bunch of canned ingredients, even though that's one of its shortcuts. I like to make a fun spread of DIY toppings, so people can choose from avocado, pico de gallo, green onions, cilantro, cheese, and sour cream—and tortilla strips (homemade or store bought) are a must! These garnishes makes the entire dish fresh and bright.

In a dutch oven or large heavy-bottomed pot, heat the oil over medium heat. Add the cumin seeds, serranos, and white and pale green parts of the green onions. Let splutter for a few seconds, then add the onions and salt. Cook for 10 to 12 minutes, stirring occasionally and scraping up any browned bits, until the onions are golden brown.

Add the tomato paste, taco seasoning, oregano, coriander, and garlic, and stir for 1 to 2 minutes, until the garlic is fragrant, but not browned. Add the tomatoes, cilantro, green chiles, adobo, pinto beans, and broth and mix well. Cover the pot and simmer over low heat for 20 minutes.

Remove 1½ cups (360 ml) of the soup and place it in a blender. Carefully blend the soup until smooth and return it to the pot, stirring to incorporate.

Add the dark green parts of the green onions and stir well. Adjust for salt. Serve with the optional garnishes.

SALADS

Growing up, salads were never really presented as a meal. We'd have plenty of veggies but not in the traditional leafy green sort of way. We'd have sides of cucumbers and tomatoes with our meals, but most of our vegetables were cooked and served warm. Now, salads are what I survive on during the week for quick lunches and dinners.

These killer vegetarian salads offer something for everyone because they are totally customizable. Not a fan of kale? Arugula too peppery for you? Go ahead and replace with a green you *do* like. I find people often get caught up when they don't like a certain ingredient or type of dressing in a salad, so I encourage you to make swaps, or mix and match dressings with different salads. There are no rules when it comes to these combos! The only thing to think about is, *Do I like these flavors and textures together?* If you do, go for it!

These super versatile salads can be served as a meal (Cold Noodle Salad with Spicy Peanut Dressing [page 80] and Taco "Salad" with Buttermilk Ranch Dressing [page 92]); a side (Smashed Potato Salad with Green Goddess Dressing [page 76], Kale & Quinoa Salad with Roasted Cauliflower, Apples & Curry Vinaigrette [page 79]); or a first course (Chopped Kachumber Salad with Spiced Sourdough Croutons [page 83] and Arugula & Spiced Lentil Salad with Balsamic-Tahini Dressing & Chili Naan Crisps [page 84]). It all depends on what you add to them (or take away). They offer savory elements, sometimes balanced with a hint of sweet fruit or a savory nut for crunch factor. Some offer lots of greens or grains. They are all on the heartier side, but if you want extra substance, add more grains (couscous and quinoa are my favorites) plus chicken, fish, meat, beans, or chickpeas for a fully satisfying entrée.

Oh, and did I mention the dressings? They are what truly makes each dish! Now before you say, *Wait, you want me to* make *this and not buy it in a bottle?* I will show you that making a dressing from scratch, and having it come together quickly, really is doable—promise!

Most of these dressings have uber-flavor, so a little bit goes a long way. Use as much as you like and store the leftovers. Double a batch and keep for up to a week in the refrigerator as dipping sauces. Try the green goddess dressing (see page 76) with a crudités board, or the curry vinaigrette (see page 79) spooned over roasted vegetables and meats.

When it comes to serving salads, instead of wasting any leftover greens that have been tossed with dressing, toss only a portion of the salad, and add more as needed. Or serve the different ingredients as a composed salad, grouping each item in its own space on a large platter, all served with dressing on the side.

SMASHED POTATO SALAD

with GREEN GODDESS DRESSING

Serves 4

For the dressing

- ½ cup (120 ml) mayonnaise
- ½ cup (120 ml) buttermilk
- 10 fresh basil leaves
- ¼ cup (11 g) roughly chopped fresh chives
- ¼ cup (13 g) roughly chopped fresh tarragon
- ¼ cup (13 g) roughly chopped fresh parsley
- 2 tablespoons roughly chopped fresh dill
- 3 cloves garlic, peeled
- ¼ teaspoon salt
- 1½ teaspoons honey
- 1 tablespoon white vinegar

For the spicy smashed potatoes

- 4 tablespoons (60 ml) extra-virgin olive oil
- 1½ teaspoons salt
- 1½ pounds (680 g) baby creamer potatoes
- ¼ teaspoon red chili powder
- 1 teaspoon garlic powder
- ¼ teaspoon ground cumin
- ¼ teaspoon ground coriander

For the salad

- 2 hearts romaine, cut or torn into small pieces
- Salt and freshly ground black pepper
- ¼ cup (30 g) radishes, cut into 1-inch (2.5 cm) matchsticks
- ⅓ cup (35 g) thinly sliced red onion
- ⅓ cup (50 g) crumbled feta cheese

While I love my greens, sometimes there's nothing better than when they take a back seat to the buttery yumminess of baby creamer potatoes, which are golf ball–size and have very thin skin and a creamy inner consistency. Here, they are prepared soft on the inside, crispy on the outside, and smashed to create as much surface area as possible to soak up all that delicious green goddess dressing, which adds just the right amount of acidity to balance the richness of the potatoes. To give this salad even more herby goodness, after making the dressing I throw any leftover herbs into the salad. The crumbled feta adds a salty, tangy accent to the dish that sends this absolutely over the top! The spice blend, dressing, and garnishes can all be made a few hours ahead (refrigerate dressing and garnish until ready to serve).

MAKE THE DRESSING: In a blender, combine the mayonnaise, buttermilk, basil, chives, tarragon, parsley, dill, garlic, salt, honey, and vinegar and blend until smooth. Refrigerate until ready to serve.

MAKE THE SPICY SMASHED POTATOES: Preheat the oven to 425°F (220°C). Coat a large rimmed baking sheet with 2 tablespoons of the oil.

Fill a large pot with water, add 1 teaspoon of the salt, and bring to a boil. Reduce the heat to a simmer, add the potatoes, and cook until fork-tender, 15 to 20 minutes.

While the potatoes are cooking, combine the chili powder, garlic powder, cumin, coriander, and remaining ½ teaspoon salt in a small bowl.

Drain the potatoes, and with a paper towel or kitchen towel, dry them, and transfer to the prepared baking sheet. While the potatoes are still warm, use the bottom of a lightly oiled drinking glass to gently smash each potato flat and even. With a pastry brush coat the tops of the potatoes with the remaining 2 tablespoons oil and sprinkle evenly with half of the spice blend, then flip the potatoes and evenly sprinkle with the remaining spice blend.

Bake the potatoes until golden brown and crispy, about 35 minutes, carefully turning the potatoes over with a spatula midway through baking.

ASSEMBLE THE SALAD: Toss ½ cup of the dressing with the romaine and season with salt and pepper to taste. Arrange the lettuce on the bottom of a large serving platter. Top with half the radishes and half the onion, then top with the smashed potatoes, feta, and the rest of the radishes and onions. Drizzle more dressing on top or serve it on the side and enjoy!

KALE & QUINOA SALAD

with ROASTED CAULIFLOWER, APPLES & CURRY VINAIGRETTE

Serves 4

For the vinaigrette

- 3 tablespoons extra-virgin olive oil
- 2 teaspoons Dijon mustard
- 2 teaspoons honey
- 2 teaspoons apple cider vinegar
- 1 clove garlic, grated
- ¼ teaspoon curry powder
- ¼ teaspoon salt

  Freshly ground black pepper

For the cauliflower

- 1 medium cauliflower (about 1½ pounds/680 g)
- 1 teaspoon garlic powder
- 1 teaspoon salt

  Freshly ground black pepper

- ¾ teaspoon curry powder
- 2 tablespoons extra-virgin olive oil
- ⅓ cup (50 g) grated Pecorino Romano cheese

For the quinoa

- 1 teaspoon extra-virgin olive oil
- ¼ teaspoon crushed red pepper
- 1 clove garlic, peeled
- ½ cup (85 g) uncooked quinoa
- 1 teaspoon salt

For the salad

- 1 bunch Tuscan kale, stems removed, leaves rolled into logs and cut into thin, short ribbons (about 4 cups/270 g)
- ½ apple, cored, halved, and thinly sliced
- ⅓ cup (45 g) pomegranate seeds

This is one of my go-to salads because it's super tasty and super flexible. Kale and quinoa provide the perfect base for whatever roasted veggies you have on hand. And while this dish tastes great with cauliflower, you can swap it out for broccoli or sweet potatoes. You can also swap out the Pecorino Romano for goat cheese or feta, and toss in whatever nuts or seeds you like for some crunch. Unlike most greens, kale doesn't wilt easily and keeps its bite even after being dressed, so I often make the kale and quinoa base and keep it in the fridge as meal prep for the week!

MAKE THE VINAIGRETTE: Whisk together the oil, mustard, honey, vinegar, garlic, curry powder, salt, and pepper in a bowl. Set aside.

Preheat the oven to 425°F (220°C).

MAKE THE CAULIFLOWER: Trim the head and break it into large florets; slice each of the florets about ¼-inch (6 mm) thick so at least one side of every floret is flat. Place in a large mixing bowl and add the garlic powder, salt, pepper, curry powder, and olive oil. Mix until the cauliflower is well coated with the spices.

Transfer the cauliflower to a baking sheet (set the bowl with the remaining oil and seasonings aside) and roast for about 25 minutes, until slightly browned and fork-tender. Remove from the oven and sprinkle generously with half of the Pecorino Romano.

MAKE THE QUINOA: Heat the oil in a saucepan over medium-high heat. Add the crushed red pepper and garlic and cook for 1 minute, until the garlic is fragrant. Add the quinoa, and cook for about 2 minutes, stirring occasionally, until nutty and fragrant, then add 1 cup (240 ml) water and the salt. Bring to a boil and cover, reduce the heat to a simmer, and cook for about 15 minutes, until the water is absorbed and the quinoa is fluffy. Set aside to cool.

ASSEMBLE THE SALAD: Add the kale, quinoa, and vinaigrette to the same bowl that was used to prepare the cauliflower and toss to combine. Transfer the salad to a serving platter or a serving bowl and top with the remaining Pecorino Romano, then add the roasted cauliflower on top, wedge in the apple slices, sprinkle with the pomegranate seeds, and serve.

COLD NOODLE SALAD

with SPICY PEANUT DRESSING

Serves 4

For the dressing

- ½ cup (120 ml) creamy peanut butter
- 3 cloves garlic, peeled
- 2 teaspoons peeled and grated fresh ginger
- 2 tablespoons soy sauce
- 2 tablespoons sriracha sauce
- 2 tablespoons honey
- 3 tablespoons (45 ml) cold water, or more if needed
- ¾ teaspoon salt
- ½ cup (20 g) roughly chopped fresh cilantro (leaves and tender stems)
- Juice of 1 lime

For the salad

- 3 ounces (85 g) dried soba noodles, cooked according to package directions
- ½ bunch Tuscan kale, center ribs removed, leaves rolled into logs and sliced into long, thin ribbons (about 2 cups/135 g)
- 1 (6-ounce/170 g) package cabbage and carrot coleslaw blend (about 1½ cups)
- 1 red bell pepper, thinly sliced
- ½ cup (75 g) roasted peanuts, crushed coarsely, 1 tablespoon reserved for garnish
- 1 jalapeño chile, seeded and thinly sliced
- 1 cup (155 g) frozen shelled edamame
- ¼ cup (15 g) sliced green onions (green parts only), plus more for garnish
- 2 tablespoons finely chopped fresh mint leaves, plus sliced mint leaves for garnish
- Lime wedges, for serving

I don't care what anyone says, noodles (when cold or at room temp) *totally* count as a salad! And here, soba noodles are paired up with lots of crunchy veggies and dark leafy greens so it *more* than counts. With all the julienned veggies (you get to take a shortcut and use a bag of premade coleslaw fixings), slices of green onion, and ribbon-like strips of kale, this veggie kaleidoscope reminds me of a spiralized salad. It can all be made ahead, tossed together in advance, and then all you have to do is mix in the peanut dressing right before serving (or serve on the side if anyone has a nut allergy). If you want a heartier salad, add some firm tofu, sliced grilled chicken, steak, or shrimp.

MAKE THE DRESSING: In a small food processor or blender, combine the peanut butter, garlic, ginger, soy sauce, sriracha, honey, cold water, salt, cilantro, and lime juice. Mix until smooth and creamy, adding more cold water a tablespoon at a time if the dressing is too thick.

MAKE THE SALAD: In a large bowl combine the noodles, kale, coleslaw blend, bell pepper, peanuts, jalapeño, edamame, sliced green onions, and chopped mint and toss to mix. Add the dressing and use tongs to combine. Garnish with the reserved peanuts and additional sliced green onions and sliced mint leaves and serve with lime wedges.

CHOPPED KACHUMBER SALAD

with SPICED SOURDOUGH CROUTONS

Serves 4

For the croutons

- 2 tablespoons extra-virgin olive oil
- ½ teaspoon red chili powder
- ½ teaspoon garlic powder
- ¼ teaspoon ground turmeric
- ½ teaspoon salt
- 1 fresh or day-old sourdough baguette, cut into ½-inch (12 mm) cubes (about 4 cups/150 g)

For the salad

- 1 tablespoon extra-virgin olive oil
- 2 teaspoons fresh lemon juice, plus more if needed
- ½ teaspoon ground cumin
- ¼ teaspoon red chili powder
- ¼ teaspoon chaat masala
- 1 teaspoon salt, plus more if needed
- ⅓ cup (40 g) finely diced onion
- 2 Persian cucumbers, diced
- 2 plum tomatoes, diced
- ½ cup (85 g) peeled and diced slightly ripe mango
- 1 (15½-ounce/445 g) can chickpeas, rinsed and drained
- 2 tablespoons finely chopped fresh cilantro

Growing up, my mom served a side of kachumber—a salad of cucumbers, tomatoes, and onion—every time we ate dal and rice. This version, with the addition of chickpeas, mango, and homemade croutons, is worthy of being enjoyed all on its own! It's bright and refreshing, and instead of a fussy vinaigrette or dressing, a simple touch of spices and salt helps bring out the natural flavors in this dish. The salad is best mixed about 20 minutes before serving, so the flavors meld and the bread softens and soaks them up. You can play with the proportions here and adjust the salt, spices, and acid to your liking. Often I up the quantity of fruit for my kids. If heirloom tomatoes are gorgeous and in season, I love to include a variety of them for their color and juiciness, and in the winter, I sometimes swap the lime for oranges or blood oranges. This salad is also improved by a handful of fresh herbs—so toss in those extra bits of mint or dill you might have in the fridge.

Preheat the oven to 350°F (175°C). Line a baking sheet with foil.

MAKE THE CROUTONS: In a large bowl, combine the oil, chili powder, garlic powder, turmeric, and salt. Add the cubed bread and stir to evenly combine. Transfer the croutons to the prepared sheet pan (save the bowl) and bake for 5 to 7 minutes, until golden brown and crispy on the outide but slightly soft in the center. Fresh bread will take slightly longer to toast than day-old.

FIFTEEN MINUTES BEFORE SERVING, MAKE THE SALAD: In the same bowl you prepared the croutons, add the oil, lemon juice, cumin, chili powder, chaat masala, and salt and stir to evenly distribute. Add the onion, cucumbers, tomatoes, mango, chickpeas, and cilantro. Toss to coat and let sit for 15 minutes. The salt will draw some liquid from the veggies and increase the flavor of the salad. Add the croutons to the salad and taste and add a bit more lemon or salt if needed. Serve on a large platter or salad bowl.

ARUGULA & SPICED LENTIL *SALAD*

with BALSAMIC-TAHINI DRESSING & CHILI NAAN CRISPS

Serves 4 to 6

For the dressing

- ½ cup (120 ml) tahini
- ¼ teaspoon salt
- 2 teaspoons Dijon mustard
- 6 tablespoons (90 ml) hot water
- 2 teaspoons fresh lemon juice
- 2 tablespoons balsamic vinegar
- 1 tablespoon extra-virgin olive oil
- 1 tablespoon honey

For the crisps

- 1 teaspoon garlic powder
- ½ teaspoon red chili powder
- ¼ teaspoon chaat masala
- ⅛ teaspoon salt
- 3 pieces naan
- 2 to 3 tablespoons canola oil, for brushing

For the lentils

- 1 cup (190 g) uncooked green lentils
- 3 tablespoons extra-virgin olive oil
- 1 tablespoon za'atar
- 1 teaspoon ground cumin
- 1 teaspoon ground coriander
- 1 lemon
- 1 teaspoon salt, plus more if needed

For the salad

- 3 cups loosely packed (70 g) arugula, roughly chopped
- 3 Persian cucumbers, diced
- 1½ cups (220 g) red seedless grapes, halved
- 2½ tablespoons finely chopped fresh parsley
- 2 tablespoons finely chopped fresh mint
- 2 tablespoons coarsely chopped fresh dill
- ⅓ cup (45 g) roasted, salted, hulled sunflower seeds
- 1 teaspoon za'atar

This is one of my favorite salads because it doesn't require that much effort, but is still filled with contrasting textures, fresh herby flavors, and a good amount of fiber and plant protein from the lentils. The grapes release a juicy, sweet burst that's unexpected and offers the perfect balance to the pepperiness of the arugula. Za'atar, an herby Middle Eastern spice blend, is used to flavor both the salad and the lentils. Try this recipe for a super satisfying packed lunch; just keep the lentils and greens separate, tossing them together only when you're ready to eat. This salad is also impressive looking when you serve it on a platter, with all the ingredients layered. You can assemble the salad ahead of time and add the sunflower seeds and dressing right before serving. It also pairs well with grilled salmon or shrimp.

MAKE THE DRESSING: In a medium bowl, whisk together the tahini, salt, mustard, hot water, lemon juice, balsamic, oil, and honey until well combined. Taste for salt and lemon and adjust the balance if necessary. If the dressing is too thick, add a bit of warm water to thin it out.

MAKE THE CRISPS: Preheat the oven to 400°F (205°C). Line a baking sheet with parchment or foil.

Combine the garlic powder, chili powder, chaat masala, and salt in a small bowl. Brush each side of the naan with the oil, and evenly sprinkle the spice blend on both sides.

Using a knife or kitchen scissors, cut the naan into long, narrow bite-size wedges or triangles. Place them in a single layer on the prepared baking sheet and bake until golden and crisp, 8 to 10 minutes, turning them over midway through baking. Transfer the chips to a cooling rack. They will crisp up further as they cool.

MAKE THE LENTILS: Combine the lentils with 5 cups (1.2 L) water in a medium saucepan and bring to a boil. Reduce the heat and simmer until the lentils are tender but still maintain their shape, 25 to 30 minutes. Drain the lentils into a large bowl, add the oil, za'atar, cumin, coriander, zest of ½ of the lemon and the juice of the whole lemon, and salt and stir well to combine.

ASSEMBLE THE SALAD: Place the arugula in a large salad bowl or on a large serving platter and top with layers of the lentils, cucumbers, and grapes. Evenly sprinkle with the parsley, mint, dill, sunflower seeds, and za'atar. Drizzle with the dressing or serve it on the side. Arrange the naan crisps around the salad platter or bowl, or in a separate dish and serve.

SUNDAY FUNDAY

Sunday Fundays make the weekend last longer, help fight the Sunday scaries, and ensure you are in bed by a decent time. A Sunday Funday means we're hanging out, it's gonna be super chill, and there will be a lot of food.

I don't like for these kind of get-togethers to be fussy, so while a magazine-worthy tablescape complete with chargers and tapered candles has its place, I much prefer friends and family hovering around the kitchen island, no matter how many times I tell them to grab a plate and sit down. When it comes to planning the menu, I like to make a couple things that can be out when people arrive, plus something hot and fresh that I serve, and some things I pick up from our favorite local restaurants, because this is real life, after all.

I won't fool you into thinking it's effortless, because the truth is, teamwork makes the dream work. Over the years, our friends and family have learned exactly where to step in and start helping when they come over. Someone will shred cheese for the barbecue paneer pizzas, another friend gets right to squeezing limes for margs, and bless their souls, some of my friends love to clean up afterward! I find that even when we have some new additions to the crew, letting them pitch in to help make a batch of cocktails or even bring desserts (because I never opt to bake) makes them feel included and right at home, which is exactly how I want everyone to feel when they're in my kitchen.

So, here's a spread that is exactly what you'll find if you showed up at my house for Sunday Funday. No fancy themes, no fuss—just food, family, and friends.

Barbecue Paneer Pizzas 88

Spiced Turkey Burgers with Tandoori Onions
& Cilantro Jalapeño Sauce 91

Taco "Salad" with Buttermilk Ranch Dressing 92

Paneer & Amul Cheese Spring Rolls 97

Spicy Watermelon Margs 101

Crudités spread—with Tarragon Aioli (256)
and Harissa Hummus (237), served with pita chips, cucumber
spears, watermelon radishes, baby carrots, etc.

BARBECUE PANEER PIZZAS

Serves 4

These BBQ paneer pizzas, with their sweet, smoky, and spicy flavors, remind me of "chili paneer," a super popular Indo-Chinese dish. This much easier version takes advantage of store-bought barbecue sauce, which I doctor up by adding lots of spices. I also take another shortcut by using ready-made naan versus homemade pizza dough. Kudos to the people who make fresh dough on a weeknight, but I am not one of them, LOL. If you've been a longtime follower of *The Chutney Life* blog, you're already fully aware of my obsession with thecha chutney, a spicy red chili garlic paste that I mix into just about anything but mainly into mayo or cream cheese, because it makes a perfect aioli for sandwiches or spread inside of quesadillas, and in this case a pizza base! If you can't find thecha chutney at your local South Asian market or online, you can make a homemade version called Lasanyu Marchu (page 263). If neither is an option, you can use sriracha or harissa sauce in their place. You can also double the barbecue sauce recipe to have an extra batch in the fridge and toss it with rotisserie chicken for a non-veg version of this pizza that would also be super delicious!

⅔ cup (155 g) cream cheese, at room temperature

1 tablespoon prepared thecha chutney or Lasanyu Marchu (page 263)

2 tablespoons canola or vegetable oil, plus more for brushing the naan

1 red onion, half diced, half thinly sliced

2 teaspoons minced garlic

1 teaspoon ground coriander

1 teaspoon ground cumin

½ teaspoon garam masala

1 teaspoon red chili powder

½ teaspoon ground turmeric

¼ teaspoon salt

1½ cups (360 ml) prepared barbecue sauce (I like Sweet Baby Ray's)

1 pound (455 g) paneer, cut into small cubes

2 tablespoons finely chopped fresh cilantro

4 pieces naan

1 pound (455 g) shredded mozzarella cheese

1 cup (90 g) sliced red bell peppers

1 cup (90 g) sliced green bell peppers

1 jalapeño, thinly sliced

½ teaspoon chaat masala

Preheat the oven to 375°F (190°C). Line two baking sheets with foil and set a rack over each tray. You can skip the racks, but they help crisp the crust.

In a small bowl, using a spoon, mix the cream cheese and the chutney until combined. Set aside.

Heat the oil in a large wide pot over medium-high. Add the diced onion and cook, stirring frequently until translucent, about 5 minutes. Add the garlic and stir until fragrant but not browned, about 30 seconds to 1 minute. Add the coriander, cumin, garam masala, chili powder, turmeric, and salt and continue to stir for about 30 seconds, until fragrant, taking care not to burn the garlic. Add the barbecue sauce and paneer and mix well. Reduce the heat to low, cover, and simmer for 8 minutes. Add the cilantro, mix well, and remove from the heat.

To assemble the pizzas, lightly brush both sides of the naan with oil and place the bread on the prepared racks or pan. Spread about 2½ tablespoons of the cream cheese mixture onto each naan, sprinkle a handful of mozzarella, and then top with 1 cup of the barbecue paneer. Add a generous quantity of the bell peppers, sliced onion, and jalapeño, based on your personal spice preference. Top with another handful of mozzarella and bake in the oven for 12 to 14 minutes, until the cheese is melted and the edges are golden. To brown the top, broil for about 1 minute on low, keeping a careful eye on it, until golden and bubbly. Remove from the oven, sprinkle each pizza with ⅛ teaspoon of chaat masala, and serve.

PRO TIP

For an extra crispy crust, I like to place the naan directly on the oven rack.

SPICED TURKEY BURGERS
with Tandoori Onions
& Cilantro Jalapeño Sauce

Serves 4

Turkey burgers can be dry and dull, but with the addition of spices, herbs, cooked onions, and my Cilantro Jalapeño Sauce, these burgers are anything but dull! The tandoori onions and the sauce can both be made ahead of time.

For the tandoori onions

1	red onion, halved and thinly sliced
2½	tablespoons unsalted butter
1½	tablespoons tandoori masala (I prefer Swad brand)

For the burgers

1	tablespoon minced garlic
1	tablespoon minced fresh ginger
2	teaspoons garam masala
1	teaspoon ground cumin
1	teaspoon garlic powder
½	teaspoon red chili powder
½	teaspoon salt
¼	cup (10 g) finely chopped fresh cilantro
1	pound (455 g) ground turkey
	Canola or vegetable oil
8	slider or hamburger rolls
8	slices pepper Jack, cheddar, or Monterey Jack cheese (optional)
	Cilantro Jalapeño Sauce (page 252)
	Lettuce and tomato, for serving

MAKE THE TANDOORI ONIONS: Add the onion, butter, and tandoori masala to a medium saucepan over medium-low heat and cook, stirring often, until the onions are softened, 15 to 20 minutes.

MAKE THE BURGERS: In a large bowl, mix together the garlic, ginger, garam masala, cumin, garlic powder, chili powder, and salt. Add the cilantro and ground turkey and mix to combine. Lightly oil your hands and form 8 burger patties, about ½ inch (12 mm) thick and 3 inches (7.5 cm) in diameter for sliders (or the size of your slider buns), or 4 larger, slightly thinner patties for regular-size burgers. Make sure the patties are level, so they cook evenly.

Add just enough oil to lightly coat a cast-iron or nonstick pan or griddle over medium-high heat. Add the burgers and cook for 5 to 7 minutes on each side, until the meat is no longer pink and the burgers are browned on both sides. If you like your rolls toasted, toast them right after you flip the burgers. If you want to make cheeseburgers, add the cheese 2 minutes before the burgers are fully cooked, and cover the pan so that the cheese melts.

TO ASSEMBLE THE BURGERS, spread the cilantro sauce on both sides of each roll and assemble the burgers with lettuce, tomato, and tandoori onions. Drizzle some extra sauce on top and serve.

TACO "SALAD"
with Buttermilk Ranch Dressing

Serves 4

This version of the Tex-Mex favorite is elevated by a tangy homemade ranch dressing that you'll want to eat with pretty much anything you find in your fridge! The dressing is best if made a few hours ahead of the salad and refrigerated, so the flavors in the dressing come together and develop.

For the dressing

- 2 cloves garlic, grated
- ¼ teaspoon salt
- ½ cup (120 ml) sour cream
- 1 cup (240 ml) mayonnaise
- ¼ cup (13 g) finely chopped fresh parsley
- 2 tablespoons finely chopped fresh chives
- 2 tablespoons finely chopped fresh dill
- ½ tablespoon apple cider vinegar or white vinegar
- 2 tablespoons taco seasoning
- 1 teaspoon ground cumin
- 1 teaspoon ground coriander
- ½ teaspoon Worcestershire sauce
- ¼ teaspoon red chili powder
- ¼ cup (60 ml) buttermilk

For the salad

- ½ red onion, finely chopped
- 1 red bell pepper, finely chopped
- 1 green bell pepper, finely chopped
- Pinch salt
- 1 (15-ounce/430 g) can black beans, drained and rinsed
- 2 romaine hearts, chopped or torn into bite-size pieces
- 2 cups (230 g) shredded pepper Jack cheese or packaged Mexican blend cheese
- ¼ cup (10 g) finely chopped fresh cilantro
- ½ head red cabbage, thinly sliced
- 2 cups (170 g) frozen corn kernels, defrosted, drained, and patted dry with paper towels
- 3 large tomatoes, chopped
- ½ cup (120 g) pickled jalapeño chiles, chopped small
- 1 ripe avocado, pitted and diced
- 3 cups (85 g) slightly crushed taco chips
- Lime wedges, for garnish

MAKE THE DRESSING: In a medium bowl, add the garlic, salt, sour cream, mayonnaise, parsley, chives, dill, vinegar, taco seasoning, cumin, coriander, Worcestershire, chili power, and buttermilk and whisk until well combined. Store in the refrigerator until ready to use.

MAKE THE SALAD: Heat a cast iron-skillet over high heat. Once the pan is hot, add the onion and red and green peppers with a pinch of salt. Do not stir. Let them sit undisturbed for 3 to 4 minutes, until they develop a nice char. Remove from the heat and toss with the beans in a bowl.

On a large platter or in a pretty glass bowl, assemble the salad by placing half of the romaine on the bottom, top with the bean mixture, then half of the cheese, and then half of the cilantro. Pour one-third of the dressing over the cheese and top with the cabbage, corn, and remaining cheese. Pour another third of the dressing over the cheese, top with the remaining romaine, tomatoes, the jalapeños, avocado, and remaining cilantro. Cover the entire salad with the crushed taco chips. Serve the extra dressing, lime wedges, and more taco chips, if desired, on the side.

PANEER & AMUL CHEESE SPRING ROLLS

Serves 6

In India, amul cheese is used in everything from dosas to fried rice to sandwiches and pastas. It's a popular cheese for its creaminess and saltiness, which makes it a great choice for adding flavor! You can find amul cheese and paneer at your local South Asian market or online. These paneer spring rolls are a breeze to put together, as the wrappers are store-bought and the cheesy creamy filling doesn't require any cooking. You can also prep these ahead, freeze them, and then fry them up when you're ready to serve. Otherwise, you can prep the filling the night before and put friends and family to work helping you fill and roll them up just before frying! Serve these with store-bought Thai sweet chili sauce or my homemade Cilantro Chutney (page 193).

7   ounces (200 g) paneer, grated on the large holes of a box grater

4   Thai green chiles, finely diced

½   large red onion, finely diced

¼   cup (10 g) finely chopped fresh cilantro

1   teaspoon cumin seeds

1   teaspoon peeled and finely grated fresh ginger

1   teaspoon crushed red pepper

⅛   teaspoon freshly ground black pepper

2   ounces (55 g) cream cheese, softened

1   cup (110 g) shredded amul cheese, grated on the large holes of a box grater

¼   teaspoon garam masala

½   teaspoon salt

2   tablespoons cornstarch

1   (14.1-ounce/400 g) package spring roll wrappers (25 wrappers)

    Canola oil

½   cup (120 ml) Thai sweet chili sauce, for serving

In a large bowl, add the paneer, chiles, onion, cilantro, cumin, ginger, crushed red pepper, black pepper, cream cheese, amul cheese, garam masala, and salt. Mix until well combined.

In a small bowl, mix the cornstarch with 3 tablespoons water and stir to form a slurry. Remove one spring roll wrapper from the package and place on the counter, oriented like a diamond, with a point (corner) facing you. Place about 2 tablespoons of the filling in the center. Fold the corner up and roll the filling away from you tightly, gently pressing down on the filling as you roll. Next, fold the left and right corners into the middle. Using your finger or a pastry brush, brush the slurry around the edges as if you are sealing an envelope, and continue rolling up the spring roll like a cigar. Repeat with the remaining wrappers and filling.

Fill a large pot with about 5 inches (12 cm) canola oil and heat over medium-high until the temperature reaches 350°F (175°C) on a candy or deep-fry thermometer. (Or, add a small roll to the hot oil; if the color is golden and the roll floats to the top immediately, the oil is ready.) Working in batches so as not to crowd the pan, fry the spring rolls for about 2 minutes per side. Place them on a paper towel–lined plate or sheet pans to drain off excess oil. Serve hot with sauce.

SPICY WATERMELON MARGS

Makes 8 drinks

Even without a juicer, watermelon has such a high water content that it makes it incredibly easy to blend and strain. Here the sweet and refreshing summer fruit is paired with tequila, lime, and spicy jalapeños—and topped off with a smoky rim of chaat masala! I make a big batch of these the night before or morning of a party and put the pitcher in the refrigerator, so they are chilled and ready to go as soon as guests arrive. You can increase the lime and agave based on how sweet or tart your watermelon is, and of course increase or decrease the tequila based on your preference. You can also omit the jalapeños if you don't like their kick.

2	quarts (2 L) fresh watermelon juice (from about ½ of a medium-size watermelon, seeds removed, blended, and strained)
20	ounces (600 ml) tequila (I prefer Casamigos)
12	ounces fresh lime juice (from 12 to 14 limes)
4	ounces (120 ml) Cointreau
6	ounces (180 ml) agave
2	jalapeño chiles, thinly sliced
1	tablespoon chaat masala
2	limes, quartered

In a large pitcher, add the watermelon juice, tequila, lime juice, Cointreau, and agave and stir to mix well. Place the jalapeños in a large glass measuring cup or Mason jar, and then pour 12 ounces (360 ml) of the margarita mixture into the jar. Using a muddler, slightly mash the jalapeños to release their heat. Strain back into the pitcher, discarding the solids, and refrigerate until chilled.

Place the chaat masala in a small dish wider than the glass's rim. Run the edge of one of the lime wedges around the rims of 8 rocks glasses, and press the rims into the chaat mixture. Fill each glass with ice and pour in the margaritas, dividing evenly among the glasses.

EASY-ISH DINNERS

I cook at least five days a week for myself and for my family, and truth be told, I make the recipes in this chapter more than any other! They are my absolute go-tos for dinner, especially during the week, as they don't require that much prep or cooking time.

Dinnertime at my house is ever-changing. One night we might be hosting my in-laws, who love my Mexican-inspired dishes, so my Black Bean Crunch Wrap Quesadillas (page 130) are often on the menu. When my cousins come over, they love the Barbecue Paneer Pizzas (page 88) and we all choose whichever toppings we like; Chandani always has to add pineapple and jalapeño to hers. When it's just the four of us, I go for something easy but still fun, such as Avocado Thecha Sandwiches (page 110) or the Veggie Hummus Sandwich (page 113) paired with a soup.

The key to weeknight meals is to have as much prepped and cooked in advance as possible. I usually take some time at the beginning of the week to peel my garlic and ginger because they're called for in so many recipes—it makes cooking every day ten times easier!

Many of the dishes in this chapter lend themselves to make-ahead mode, and some, including the One-Pan Cheesy Pav Bhaji Quinoa (page 129) and Tawa Pulao with Kidney Beans (page 133), can be frozen and reheated to get dinner on the table superfast. And if you want to be an uber-planner, use Sunday to prep meals for the rest of the week. You don't have to make everything ahead, just figure out three or four dishes you want to serve and prepare bits and pieces of them in advance. Chop an onion for a recipe you're making that day and go ahead and chop some extra for a recipe you'll make later in the week. Double a recipe on the weekend and have it for lunch or dinner again during the week.

When I come up with recipes for my blog, I like to keep in mind that everyone's threshold for meal prep, and their capacity, time, and energy, is different. With that said, while a dish like the black bean quesadillas might take more time to prepare, the beans (which can be doubled for leftovers) can be repurposed in so many different ways throughout the week—a breakfast burrito, atop a salad, alongside rice—that the extra effort actually becomes a timesaver. It's a win-win!

SANDWICH NIGHT

One of my favorite ways to entertain, and also to get dinner on the table quickly, is sandwich night. I offer three or four different types of sandwiches that feature a variety of breads, fillings, and spreads, and guests can customize their own creations. Here are a handful of popular sandwiches that I've served at many a lunch or casual dinner. Feel free to mix, match, and swap out ingredients to make them your own!

SAMOSA GRILLED CHEESE

Makes 4 sandwiches

2	tablespoons canola or vegetable oil
½	teaspoon mustard seeds
1	teaspoon cumin seeds
¼	teaspoon hing (asafetida)
1	serrano chile, finely chopped
1	small onion, finely diced
1	teaspoon salt
2	large cloves garlic, grated
1½	teaspoons ground coriander
1	teaspoon ground cumin
½	teaspoon red chili powder
¼	teaspoon ground turmeric
1	teaspoon garam masala
3	medium potatoes, peeled, boiled, and cut into small dice
8	slices sandwich bread
½	cup (120 ml) Cilantro Chutney (page 193)
½	cup (120 ml) Apple Butter Chutney (page 254)
8	slices cheese of your choice (I prefer white or yellow American cheese)
1	to 2 tablespoons unsalted butter, for the pan

PRO TIP

Spread the potato mixture over a flatbread or pizza crust, top with cheese, and bake in a preheated 375°F (190°C) oven until the flatbread or crust is warm and the bottom is crisp and the cheese is melted, 5 to 10 minutes depending on the size of your flatbread or pizza. Remove from the oven and drizzle with both of the chutneys for a samosa pizza that will wow your guests at a party!

This grilled cheese is one of the most requested lunches by everyone in my family. It's satisfying, comforting, and hits all the sweet-spicy cravings in one delicious bite. The filling in this recipe is made from potatoes and is similar to the filling found in samosas, minus the peas. You can make the filling a couple of days ahead and store it in the fridge until you're ready to use it. Having frozen cilantro and tamarind-date chutney (or my easier version, Apple Butter Chutney) on hand that you can defrost will also speed up the process of getting this meal on the table. While the kid in me loves these made with classic American cheese, feel free to swap with a more grown-up choice, such as sliced smoked Gouda, or pepper Jack!

To make the potato mixture, heat the oil in a large skillet over medium-high heat. Add the mustard seeds, cumin seeds, and hing. Once the spices begin to sizzle, add the serrano and cook for about 1 minute. Reduce the heat to medium, add the onion and salt and cook until they are translucent, about 3 minutes. Add the garlic and cook until it is fragrant, about 1 minute. Reduce the heat to medium-low, stir in the coriander, cumin, chili powder, turmeric, and garam masala and cook for 2 minutes. Add the potatoes and mix well to coat and combine them evenly with the spices. Using the back of a spoon or a potato masher, gently smash the potatoes and stir. You don't want mashed potatoes, but you don't want large chunks, either. Set the pan aside.

For each grilled cheese sandwich, spread one piece of bread with about 1 tablespoon of the cilantro chutney and the other piece with 1 tablespoon of the apple butter chutney. Place one slice of cheese on top of the cilantro chutney.

Heat a large nonstick skillet over medium-high heat, add 1 tablespoon of the butter, and carefully swirl to coat the bottom of the pan. (I make two sandwiches at a time.)

Place 2 slices of the cilantro and cheese bread, dry side down, in the pan. Top with a few spoonfuls of the potato mixture, gently press another slice of cheese on top of the potatoes, and top with the slice of bread spread with apple butter chutney, dry side up.

Cook until both sides of the bread are golden and the cheese has melted, 3 to 4 minutes. Add more butter to the pan as needed, and repeat. Serve immediately.

Avocado THECHA SANDWICH

Serves 4

- 8 slices rustic sourdough bread
- 4 tablespoons (55 g) unsalted butter
- ½ cup (120 ml) mayonnaise
- 2 teaspoons thecha chutney, or more to taste
- 3 ripe avocados, pitted and thinly sliced

   Salt and freshly ground black pepper

- 1 teaspoon fresh oregano, finely chopped
- 1 cup (about 85 g) sprouts (any kind)
- 4 large tomatoes, sliced
- 1 teaspoon chaat masala
- 1 red onion, very thinly sliced

This decadent sandwich is a smart way to take advantage of whatever veggies might be in your fridge. Over the years I've added everything from sliced cooked potatoes to beets to cucumbers and cabbage to this sandwich, so feel free to make it your own! Thecha is a spicy condiment made from chile peppers, garlic, and a variety of spices that lends this sandwich its unique flavor. You will always find a few packets of thecha chutney in my pantry, but if you can't track this down at your local South Asian market or online, make a batch of my Lasanyu Marchu (page 263), which makes a great swap. I love to have a batch of thecha and mayo ready to go in my fridge to put on burgers and inside grilled cheese for some added oomph.

Toast the bread and lightly butter each slice. In a small bowl, mix the mayonnaise and the thecha chutney and spread it on each slice of bread, on top of the butter. Set 4 slices aside to top the sandwiches.

Begin to layer the sandwich fillings by shingling the avocado slices over the mayonnaise, and lightly seasoning them with salt, black pepper, and about half of the oregano. Top with the sprouts, 2 or 3 slices of tomato, and a sprinkle of the chaat masala. Top with the red onion and the remaining chaat and oregano, a pinch of salt, and some freshly ground pepper. Place the reserved slices of bread on top, mayonnaise side down, and serve.

VEGGIE HUMMUS SANDWICH

Serves 4

8 slices bread of your choice

1 cup (240 ml) Cilantro Jalapeño Hummus (page 237; see Pro Tip)

1½ to 2 cups loosely packed (30 to 40 g) arugula

2 tomatoes, thinly sliced

2 small Persian or mini cucumbers, or half a cucumber, thinly sliced

1 small red onion, thinly sliced

1 cup (90 g) peppadew peppers, drained, patted dry, and thinly sliced

½ cup (75 g) crumbled feta cheese

PRO TIP

If you don't want to make the hummus from scratch, you can just add a diced jalapeño and a handful of any sort of fresh herbs to store-bought hummus and blend until creamy and smooth!

This veggie-filled sandwich is my take on Panera's Mediterranean Veg Sandwich, which I order every time I go there, oftentimes making a special trip in that direction just to eat one! This recipe is super flexible and tastes great on any type of bread, including ciabatta, multigrain, olive bread, and baguettes. When it comes to the filling, don't feel you have to be exact with the measurements. It's all about what's readily available, or what you're in the mood for. Love sweet and spicy peppadews? Add extra. Don't have any? Swap them out for sweet pickled cherry peppers. If it's tomato season, take advantage of that! And add some homegrown basil or other fresh herbs if you have them. The possibilities are endless and the bulk of the flavor here comes from the delicious Cilantro Jalapeño Hummus (page 237), so start with that for the prep!

Lightly toast the bread. Lay out the slices of bread and spread the hummus evenly on all 8 slices. Set 4 slices aside to top the sandwiches. On the remaining 4 slices, evenly divide and layer the arugula, tomatoes, cucumbers, onion, and peppadew peppers and top with feta cheese. Place the reserved slices of bread on top, hummus side down, slice in half on the diagonal, and serve.

CAULIFLOWER TOASTIES

with WHIPPED GOAT CHEESE

Serves 4

For the goat cheese spread

- 2 ounces (55 g) cream cheese, softened
- 2 ounces (55 g) goat cheese or feta, softened
- 1 tablespoon extra-virgin olive oil
- 3 cloves garlic, peeled and roughly chopped

  Generous pinch crushed red pepper

  Salt and freshly ground black pepper

For the cauliflower

- 2 tablespoons extra-virgin olive oil
- 1 teaspoon mustard seeds
- ½ teaspoon cumin seeds
- ⅛ teaspoon hing (asafetida)
- 5 cups (675 g) small cauliflower florets (from 1½ heads)
- ¾ teaspoon salt
- ½ teaspoon ground turmeric
- 1 teaspoon red chili powder
- ¼ teaspoon ground coriander
- ½ teaspoon ground cumin
- ¼ cup (60 ml) water or vegetable broth
- ½ cup (75 g) peas
- 3 tablespoons finely chopped fresh cilantro, plus more for garnish

- 3 tablespoons unsalted butter
- 4 to 6 slices crusty bread (I prefer sourdough)

  Extra-virgin olive oil, for serving

  Crushed red pepper, for garnish

I'm a sucker for any sort of open-face toastie or melt, or basically anything that gets served on a delicious piece of sourdough. These cauliflower toasties are inspired by fulevar and vatana nu shaak, a traditional vegetable dish of cauliflower and peas that I ate growing up, with a side of roti. This is the fun version, with a whipped goat cheese spread that adds the perfect tang and creaminess to the smoky and earthy flavors of the spiced cauliflower. This recipe can be spun into so many variations. If you've got some frozen naan on hand, you can make a quick wrap filled with these toppings or use them to top to a naan pizza. If you don't care for goat cheese, you can swap it for more cream cheese or use feta.

MAKE THE GOAT CHEESE SPREAD: Combine the cream cheese, goat cheese, oil, garlic, and crushed red pepper in a small food processor and blend until smooth. Season with salt and pepper as needed.

MAKE THE CAULIFLOWER: Heat the oil in a wide-bottomed pot with a lid or dutch oven over medium-high heat. Add the mustard seeds and when they begin to sizzle, after about 30 seconds, add the cumin seeds and hing and stir for 1 minute. Add the cauliflower florets, salt, turmeric, chili powder, coriander, and cumin and stir well. Add the water, cover, reduce the heat to medium-low, and continue to cook for 10 minutes, stirring occasionally. Add the peas and cilantro and check the cauliflower. It should be fork-tender with a bit of bite, not mushy. Continue to cook for a few more minutes, if needed.

Meanwhile, melt the butter in a large skillet over medium-high heat and, working in batches if necessary, toast the bread in the butter until slightly golden, 2 to 3 minutes per side. Spread each piece of bread with a generous schmear of the whipped goat cheese, top with a few spoonfuls of the cauliflower, sprinkle with fresh cilantro, drizzle with extra-virgin olive oil, and garnish with a pinch of crushed red pepper, if desired.

PRO TIP

To get nice, long, elegant veggie strips, use an inexpensive but effective Y-shape vegetable peeler. Shave down one side of the vegetable; when you get to the center of it, turn it over on your cutting board and shave down the other side. Stack the strips and carefully slice lengthwise into narrower strips.

Shiitake Mushroom CHEESESTEAKS

with SRIRACHA AIOLI & PICKLED VEGGIES

Serves 4, generously

For the pickled veggies

- 2 Persian cucumbers, shaved and cut into long strips (see Pro Tip)
- 1 medium carrot, peeled, shaved, and cut into long strips (see Pro Tip)
- 2 tablespoons finely chopped fresh cilantro
- 1 teaspoon sugar
- ¼ cup (60 ml) rice wine vinegar
- ¼ teaspoon coriander seeds, crushed
- 5 black peppercorns
- 1 teaspoon salt, plus more if needed after pickling

For the sandwiches

- 3 tablespoons canola or vegetable oil
- 1 red bell pepper, sliced into 1½-inch (4 cm) strips
- 9 cups (765 g) sliced shiitake mushrooms (about 1½ pounds/680 g)
- 1 tablespoon minced garlic
- ¾ teaspoon salt
- 2 teaspoons soy sauce
- 1 teaspoon onion powder
- 1 teaspoon crushed red pepper
- 4 to 6 slices cheese (I love Cooper's sharp cheese, pepper Jack, or American), plus more as desired
- 4 to 6 tablespoons unsalted butter, softened
- 4 (6-inch/15 cm) hoagie rolls
- 1 cup (240 ml) Sriracha Aioli (page 256)

Philly is known for its awesome cheesesteaks. I've tried a bunch of them, but they don't hold a candle to this vegetarian version. I like to make a double batch of Sriracha Aioli (page 256), because it so versatile. This recipe calls for a pound and a half of shiitake mushrooms, which can be pricey. It definitely may be worth heading to your local South Asian market to try to find them for less.

MAKE THE PICKLED VEGGIES: In a Mason jar with a lid or a tightly sealed container, combine the cucumbers, carrot, cilantro, sugar, vinegar, coriander, peppercorns, and salt. Refrigerate for at least 1 hour. Taste and add more salt, if desired.

MAKE THE SANDWICHES: Heat 1 tablespoon of the oil in a large skillet over medium-high. Add the bell pepper to the pan, spreading it out evenly in one layer. Let cook undisturbed for about 3 minutes, allowing it to get slightly charred, then toss and cook undisturbed for an additional 2 minutes. Transfer to a plate.

Add the remaining 2 tablespoons oil and the mushrooms to the skillet. Cook for 2 to 3 minutes, until the mushrooms are glossy and fork-tender.

Return the bell pepper to the pan, along with the garlic, salt, soy sauce, onion powder, and crushed red pepper and cook for an additional 2 to 3 minutes, until the garlic is fragrant and the liquid released from the bell pepper and mushrooms has cooked off. Reduce the heat slightly, place the cheese slices evenly over the mushrooms and bell pepper, being careful to keep the cheese slices from touching so they're not difficult to separate for individual sandwiches, and cover, allowing the cheese to melt.

Preheat the broiler.

Spread the butter on the cut side of rolls, dividing it evenly, and broil the rolls for 1 to 2 minutes, keeping a careful eye on them, until the outsides are crisp and the insides are golden (this is important so you don't end up with a soggy cheesesteak). Remove from the broiler and spread the sriracha aioli on the cut sides of the rolls.

Top the rolls with the bell pepper, mushrooms, and cheese mixture. Melt more cheese on the remaining mushrooms as desired to make more sandwiches. Tuck some of the pickled veggies into each cheesesteak and serve immediately.

HANGOVER SPAGHETTI, PAGE 120

HANGOVER SPAGHETTI

Serves 4

1 pound (455 g) spaghetti

½ cup (120 ml) extra-virgin olive oil

10 cloves garlic, thinly sliced

1 teaspoon crushed red chili peppers

1 cup (240 ml) arrabbiata sauce (I prefer Rao's)

1 teaspoon salt

½ cup (50 g) grated Pecorino Romano, plus more for serving

½ teaspoon freshly ground black pepper

Juice of ½ lemon

⅓ cup (17 g) finely chopped fresh parsley

Handful torn fresh basil leaves

You know how when you're feeling hungover, all your body wants is carbs, but the idea of cooking something seems way too overwhelming? Well this pasta dish is more about assembling than cooking, so your overserved body and brain will thank you!

Bring a large pot of salted water to boil. Add the spaghetti, cook according to package directions, and drain.

Heat the oil in a large skillet with high sides over low heat. Add the garlic and crushed red pepper and cook for 1 or 2 minutes, stirring, taking care not to let the garlic get too dark. Add the sauce and stir for 1 minute. Add the salt, Pecorino Romano, cooked spaghetti, black pepper, lemon juice, and parsley and stir to combine. Taste, adjust seasoning as needed, and garnish with basil. Serve with additional cheese.

MASALA POT PIES

Serves 4

1½ cups (360 ml) vegetable broth

1 cup (240 ml) whole milk

2 tablespoons unsalted butter

1 cup (110 g) diced onion

1 cup (140 g) diced carrots

1 cup (100 g) diced celery

2 medium Yukon gold potatoes, peeled and diced (about 1½ cups/215 g)

1 teaspoon salt

1 tablespoon minced garlic

2 teaspoons ground cumin

2 teaspoons ground coriander

2 teaspoons red chili powder

2 teaspoons Cajun seasoning

1 teaspoon ground turmeric

1 teaspoon garam masala

¼ cup (30 g) all-purpose flour

½ cup (75 g) fresh or frozen peas

½ cup (75 g) fresh or frozen corn kernels

2 teaspoons Worcestershire sauce

4 ounces (115 g) Gruyère, grated (about 1 cup)

2 ounces (55 g) Fontina, grated (about ½ cup)

¼ cup (10 g) chopped fresh cilantro

Salt, if needed

1 sheet puff pastry, thawed in the refrigerator

1 large egg and ½ teaspoon water, beaten to form an egg wash

There is something SO satisfying about a pot pie. The creaminess from Gruyère and Fontina paired with smoky spices such as coriander and cumin—it's the stuff of dreams! You definitely won't miss the meat in this vegetarian version. I find making these in individual ramekins is the best route because it helps keep the puff pastry from getting too stretched out and soggy. Switch up the vegetables in this dish based on the season! In the spring and summer months, take advantage of fresh peas and crisp asparagus. In the fall and winter, you can add butternut squash and hearty kale.

Preheat the oven to 375°F (190°C).

In a small pot, combine the vegetable broth and milk and warm over low heat.

In a large saucepan or dutch oven, melt the butter over medium-low heat. Add the onion, carrots, celery, potatoes, and salt. Cook, stirring occasionally, until the vegetables are tender, about 8 minutes. Add the garlic and stir until fragrant, about 2 minutes. Add the cumin, coriander, chili powder, Cajun seasoning, turmeric, garam masala, and flour and stir to coat the vegetables.

Increase the heat to medium, and slowly add the vegetable broth mixture in small increments, using a wooden spoon or spatula to scrape up any browned bits on the bottom of the pan. Switch to a whisk and continue to add the liquid, allowing the sauce to thicken. After a few minutes, add the peas and corn.

Bring to a simmer and let the mixture cook for 3 to 4 minutes, until it has thickened slightly. Reduce the heat to low, stir in the Worcestershire, and gradually stir in the cheeses. Add the cilantro and taste for salt. Turn off the heat and set the filling aside.

continues

NOTE

You will need four 1½ cup (360 ml) ovenproof ramekins or soup dishes to make individual pot pies, or an 8-inch (20 cm) square baking dish to make one large pot pie.

Remove the thawed puff pastry sheet from the refrigerator. Use one of the ramekins as a stencil to cut out four rounds of dough with a 1-inch (2.5 cm) overhang. Or if you are using an 8-inch (20 cm) square baking dish, trim the pastry accordingly with a 1-inch (2.5 cm) overhang.

Portion the filling into each of the ramekins or the baking dish, leaving about ½ inch (12 mm) space at the top (otherwise you will have a soggy pastry if the dough touches the filling while it bakes).

Brush the egg wash around the outside rims and a bit of the sides of the ramekins or baking dish. Place the puff pastry cutouts directly on top, folding the dough down the sides and pinching it so it stays in place during baking.

Brush each puff pastry with the egg wash and use a sharp knife to cut a slit in the center of the dough to create an escape for steam.

Place the ramekins or baking dish on a baking sheet and bake for 30 to 35 minutes, until the puff pastry is golden and cooked all the way through. Let cool for a few minutes before serving.

BUTTERY BOWTIES & MATAR

Serves 4

- 1 pound (455 g) farfalle pasta
- 6 tablespoons (85 g) unsalted butter
- 1½ cups (315 g) peas, thawed if using frozen
- 1 tablespoon minced garlic
- ½ teaspoon garam masala
- ¼ teaspoon ground turmeric
- 1½ teaspoons salt, plus more for serving
- ¾ cup (180 ml) heavy cream
- ¾ cup (70 g) grated Pecorino Romano, plus extra for serving

  Freshly ground black pepper

My favorite type of food is toddler food. I say this because somehow kid food is simple and effortless, yet it is always so satisfying and comforting. It's also oftentimes quite decadent with butter, cream, and cheese—some of my favorite food groups, ha! Buttery Bowties and Matar is a riff on a quick pasta dish I've always made for Shaan, and without fail, every time I make it, Pinank and I call dibs on the leftovers. The tiniest hint of garam masala in here goes a long way, and considering this dish contains minimal ingredients, you won't want to skip it! If you don't like peas, you can swap them out for asparagus or broccoli. If you want to add protein, some grilled shrimp or chicken would be a fabulous addition.

Cook the pasta according to the package directions and drain, reserving 1 cup (240 ml) of the pasta water. Transfer the pasta to a serving bowl, toss with 2 tablespoons of the butter, and cover to keep warm while you make the sauce.

Using the same pot, heat 2 tablespoons of the butter over medium-low heat. Add the peas, garlic, garam masala, and turmeric and stir until the garlic is fragrant, about 2 minutes. Return the pasta to the pan and stir to coat evenly. Add the reserved pasta water and the salt, increase the heat slightly, and stir until most of the water has been absorbed, 3 to 4 minutes.

Add the cream and continue to stir until the mixture is creamy and clings to the pasta, 2 to 3 minutes. Turn off the heat, add the Pecorino Romano and the remaining 2 tablespoons butter, and stir. Season with salt and pepper and serve with additional cheese.

Spaghetti Squash
MASALA

Serves 4

1 large spaghetti squash, halved, seeds removed

4 tablespoons (60 ml) safflower or canola oil

Salt and freshly ground black pepper

2 tablespoons mustard seeds

1 tablespoon cumin seeds

1 red onion, finely chopped

3 cloves garlic, grated

1 (2-inch/5 cm) piece fresh ginger, peeled and grated

1 serrano chile, chopped

2 teaspoons garam masala

2 teaspoons tandoori masala

1 teaspoon ground cumin

½ cup (120 ml) tomato paste

1 cup (240 ml) vegetable broth or water

½ cup (120 ml) heavy cream

2 tablespoons unsalted butter

3 tablespoons finely chopped fresh cilantro, plus more for garnish

Grated Parmesan cheese (optional)

PRO TIP

With their tough skins, cutting winter squash can sometimes be tricky. I've found that using an offset knife—which has the blade lower than the handle, making an L-shape—with a serrated blade is helpful.

While spaghetti is my love language, I'm all for low-carb alternatives that don't compromise on flavor. After this spaghetti squash caramelizes in the oven, you end up with al dente strands of goodness that are then tossed in a rich tomato-butter sauce, so while it's not starchy like pasta, it's still very satisfying. I call for a hefty amount of mustard seeds because I love the taste and texture they provide—almost like a Bolognese sauce—but if it's not your thing, cut the amount by half. This dish looks super fancy if you serve it in the hollowed-out squash halves with a little grated Parm on top! If you want to make it heartier, try adding some chickpeas, lentils, or dark greens such as kale and spinach. It makes an excellent base for leftover mix-ins.

Preheat the oven to 375°F (190°C). Line a baking sheet with aluminum foil.

Lightly rub the outside and inside of the squash with 1 tablespoon of the oil and season both sides with salt and pepper. Place the squash cut side down on the foil and roast until the flesh is tender and the bottom edges are slightly caramelized, 45 to 50 minutes,.

Meanwhile, in a large nonstick pan or dutch oven, heat the remaining 3 tablespoons oil over medium-high heat, add the mustard seeds and cumin seeds, and cook for about 30 seconds. As the seeds begin to sizzle, add the onion and 1 teaspoon salt, reduce the heat to medium, and cook for 3 minutes, stirring occasionally. Add the garlic, ginger, and serrano and cook for about 1 minute, stirring frequently so the garlic does not brown. Stir in the garam masala, tandoori masala, cumin, and tomato paste and cook for about 30 seconds, until the paste becomes darker in color and the spices become aromatic.

Slowly stir in the broth and heavy cream and bring the mixture to a boil. Cook for 1 to 2 minutes, until the sauce is creamy. Stir in the butter and cilantro. (If you are adding any additional veggies you can add them now and simmer until they are warm.) Season with salt and pepper.

Remove the squash from the oven. Use a kitchen towel to hold the outside of the squash, and using a fork, gently rake the flesh to create the "spaghetti" and transfer to a serving bowl, or place the strands of squash back inside the hollowed-out squash shell. Top the squash with the sauce and garnish with more cilantro and some cheese if desired.

One-Pan
CHEESY PAV BHAJI QUINOA

Serves 4

- 2 tablespoons canola or vegetable oil
- 1 teaspoon cumin seeds
- 2 Thai green chiles, finely chopped
- 1 large onion, finely chopped
- 1½ teaspoons salt, plus more if needed
- 2 plum tomatoes, cored and finely chopped
- ½ cup (65 g) peas, thawed if frozen
- 1 medium potato, peeled and cut into small dice
- 1 tablespoon minced garlic
- 1 tablespoon pav bhaji masala
- ½ teaspoon ground turmeric
- 1 teaspoon red chili powder
- 1 cup (170 g) quinoa, rinsed
- 2 tablespoons unsalted butter
- 2 teaspoons fresh lemon juice
- ¾ cup (85 g) coarsely grated Monterey Jack cheese
- ¼ cup (35 g) finely diced red onion, for garnish
- ¼ cup (10 g) chopped fresh cilantro, for garnish
- Lemon wedges, for serving

Pav Bhaji, a famous street food originating in Mumbai, is made from an assortment of vegetables, usually potatoes, cauliflower, and peas, tossed in spices and butter and cooked to a luscious, silky consistency. It's perfect for scooping with big, toasty pieces of buttered buns. I swear I can turn it into a million different things: Pav Bhaji Pizza, Pav Bhaji Paninis, Pav Bhaji Eggs—endless variations! Here I kick up the protein by cooking the veggies with the quinoa, all together in one pan. Same great flavors and less cleanup! My mom would make this veggie-spice combo at home whenever she wanted to use up eggplant, bell peppers, and cabbage—basically whatever was in the fridge—so feel free to swap out the potatoes and peas for what you have on hand. And while I love the cheese on top (have I told you how much I love cheese?), making it vegan by leaving out the cheese and replacing the butter with oil is equally delicious.

In a large 12-inch (30.5 cm) oven-safe skillet, heat the oil over medium-high heat. Add the cumin seeds and chiles, and once they begin to sizzle, add the onion and salt. Reduce the heat to medium and cook until the onion is translucent and slightly golden, about 5 minutes. Add the tomatoes and cook for about 3 minutes, until soft and jammy. Add the peas, potato, garlic, pav bhaji masala, turmeric, and chili powder and stir until the garlic is fragrant but not browned, about 1 minute.

Add the quinoa and cook for about 2 minutes, stirring often. Add 3 cups (720 ml) water, stir, and bring to a boil. Cover and reduce the heat to low. Cook, covered, for 15 to 20 minutes, until about three-fourths of the liquid has been absorbed by the quinoa. Remove the lid, stir in the butter and lemon juice, and continue to cook for 5 minutes, uncovered, stirring occasionally. Taste for salt and adjust if necessary.

Set the broiler to low.

Evenly top the quinoa with the cheese, place the pan on the middle rack of the oven, and broil until the cheese is slightly browned in places. Keep an eye on it as it can burn if you step away for too long. Remove from the oven and top with red onion and cilantro, and serve with lemon wedges.

Black Bean
CRUNCH WRAP
QUESADILLAS

Makes 4 quesadillas

2 tablespoons canola or vegetable oil, plus more for pan-frying the quesadillas

½ teaspoon cumin seeds

1 jalapeño chile, finely chopped

2 cloves garlic, minced

1 (16-ounce/455 g) can refried black beans

2 teaspoons taco seasoning

½ teaspoon ground coriander

½ teaspoon ground cumin

1 cup (240 ml) store-bought salsa

Salt, if needed

4 (10-inch/25 cm) flour tortillas

1 pound (455 g) shredded Mexican blend cheese

2 crunchy taco shells, split in half

4 tablespoons (60 ml) Chipotle Aioli (page 254)

3 cups (165 g) shredded lettuce

3 plum tomatoes, diced

Pico de gallo, sliced avocado, and sour cream, for serving

When I was growing up, Taco Bell played a big part in my life. It was (and still is) one of the only fast-food restaurants that had more than just one or two vegetarian options for my family. On the rare occasion my mom was too tired to cook (and believe me that was VERY rare, indeed), a few Mexican pizzas and seven-layer burritos would be dinner, and yes, we'd bust out the giant jar of Taco Bell sauce packets from the pantry. This crunch wrap is a riff on their famous Crunch Wrap Supreme, but a lot easier to assemble since it's in quesadilla form. I like using black beans instead of pinto beans, which the sweet, spicy smoky chipotle sauce complements perfectly. Pinank always asks for more of it for dipping, so I double the batch and you might want to also! And if, like Taco Bell, you like double the crunch, you can double the taco shells!

To make the beans, heat 2 tablespoons oil in a medium saucepan over medium heat. Add the cumin seeds and let them sizzle for about 10 seconds. Add the jalapeño and garlic and stir for about 10 seconds, until the garlic is fragrant but not browned. Add the refried beans, taco seasoning, coriander, cumin, and salsa, and stir well to combine. Reduce the heat and simmer the beans for about 10 minutes, stirring occasionally. Taste for salt (store-bought taco seasoning generally has enough salt).

To assemble the quesadilla, spread a tortilla with about ⅓ cup (85 g) of the black bean mixture and top with a handful of cheese and one-half of a taco shell. Spread 1 tablespoon of the aioli over the taco shell and begin to layer the fillings, starting with a handful of shredded lettuce, tomato, and another sprinkle of cheese. Fold the other half of the tortilla over and lightly press to form a quesadilla. Continue with the remaining tortillas and filling.

Heat 1 teaspoon of oil in a large nonstick skillet over medium heat. Working in batches, carefully transfer the assembled quesadillas to the pan and cook until golden and crispy, 2 to 3 minutes on each side. Adjust the temperature as needed, so the quesadillas don't burn, and add additional oil as needed. Transfer to a serving platter. Repeat with the remaining quesadillas. Cut each quesadilla crosswise in half and serve with pico de gallo, avocado, and sour cream.

TAWA PULAO

with KIDNEY BEANS

Serves 4

- 3 tablespoons canola or vegetable oil
- 1 teaspoon cumin seeds
- 3 Thai green chiles, finely chopped
- 1 medium yellow or white onion, diced
- 1 (16-ounce/455 g) bag mixed vegetables, thawed and patted dry
- 2 tablespoons garlic, minced
- 1 tablespoon tomato paste
- 2 teaspoons salt
- 2 tablespoons pav bhaji masala
- 2 tablespoons unsalted butter
- 4 cups (700 g) cooked basmati rice, cold
- 1 (15½-ounce/455 g) can kidney beans, drained and rinsed
- ¼ cup (10 g) finely chopped fresh cilantro, plus more for garnish

  Classic Raita (page 259)

  Chaat Onions (page 260)

PRO TIP

Frozen vegetables can retain a lot of water, so be sure to thaw and dry them properly. Too much liquid will result in mushy rice. Also, leftover rice is drier than a fresh, warm batch and will result in a better, crispier fried rice, so plan ahead!

Growing up, my mom wasn't the only cook in the kitchen. My masi, my mom's sister and the youngest of seven siblings, lived with my family since I was a child. Masi literally translates into "like mother," and that's exactly what she was, just more easygoing and chill than Mom, LOL! Over the years, her specialties in the kitchen were quick-and-easy meals, as she never liked to fuss over cooking like my mom did. Her favorite thing to make was fried rice, and her tawa pulao was always in the fridge. She played around with the ingredients based on whatever we had on hand, but it was always loaded with veggies. This version that she makes with kidney beans is my favorite and something I make for myself often. It's spicy, made easy but still hearty with a bag of frozen mixed vegetables and a can of kidney beans, and a solid meal when served with some raita!

In a large wide-bottomed skillet or dutch oven, heat the oil over medium-high heat. Add the cumin seeds and once they begin to sizzle, add the chiles and cook for about 10 seconds or so. Add the onion and cook until translucent, about 5 minutes. Add the frozen mixed vegetables and cook until they begin to soften, 3 to 5 minutes.

Reduce the heat slightly and add the garlic, tomato paste, and salt and cook for about 20 seconds until the garlic is fragrant. Add the pav bhaji masala and butter and sauté the spice mix for about 20 seconds, until the butter is melted. Gently mix in the rice in a folding motion, so the grains become loose and coated but are not mushy. Once the rice is evenly coated with all of the spices, gently stir in the kidney beans and cilantro and remove from the heat. Serve warm with a side of raita and chaat onions.

Masi (maternal aunt) literally translates to "like mom," and mine is just that! I like to call her the fun mom; she is the youngest of her seven siblings and so young at heart.

TAWA PULAO, PAGE 133

Crispy Gochujang-Glazed SWEET POTATO TACOS

Serves 6

2 tablespoons gochujang (Korean chili paste)

1 tablespoon hoisin sauce

2 tablespoons prepared sweet Thai chile sauce

1 tablespoon soy sauce

3 cloves garlic, grated

1 teaspoon ground cumin

½ teaspoon salt, plus more as needed

1 teaspoon rice wine vinegar

¼ cup (10 g) finely chopped fresh cilantro

1 tablespoon plus ¼ cup (60 ml) canola or vegetable oil

2 large sweet potatoes (about 2½ pounds/1.2 kg total), peeled and cut into cubes

1 cup (150 g) kimchi, drained and chopped small

1 bunch green onions, thinly sliced

12 (6-inch/15 cm) corn tortillas

1 pound (455 g) Monterey Jack cheese, coarsely grated (about 4 cups)

Flaky sea salt, for the taco shells

Toppings

1 cup (240 ml) sour cream

¼ cup (60 ml) prepared sweet Thai chile sauce

3 tablespoons finely chopped fresh cilantro

2 serrano or jalapeño chiles, finely sliced

2 limes, quartered

When I need to get something satisfying and delicious on the table fast, these tacos deliver! Peeling and chopping sweet potatoes requires some elbow grease and takes a bit of time, so I prefer to buy pre-cut cubed sweet potatoes for this recipe. Gochujang is a Korean chili paste that brings the heat and is a handy condiment to keep in the fridge, so order some from Amazon or grab it at your local grocery store or Asian grocery store.

Preheat the oven to 425°F (220°C). Line a rimmed baking sheet with parchment paper.

In a large bowl, add the gochujang, hoisin sauce, Thai chile sauce, soy sauce, garlic, cumin, salt, rice wine vinegar, cilantro, and 1 tablespoon of the oil and stir until well combined. Add the sweet potatoes and mix gently until combined.

Spread out the sweet potato mixture on the prepared baking sheet, place on the middle rack of the oven, and roast for 30 to 35 minutes, until the sweet potatoes are fork-tender and the bottoms are golden brown. Midway through roasting, carefully flip the potatoes for even cooking. Remove the sweet potatoes from the oven, add the kimchi and green onions, and gently toss to combine.

Pour the remaining ¼ cup (60 ml) oil in a small dish and lightly brush the bottoms of the tortillas with the oil. Heat a large nonstick skillet over medium heat and add 2 tortillas, oiled sides down. Spread a handful of cheese on one-half of each of the tortillas and top with 2 spoonfuls of the sweet potato mixture, using a fork to slightly press them down and being careful not to overstuff them. Top with more cheese and fold the tacos in half to create quesadillas. Cook until golden and crisp, flipping once, for about 2 minutes per side. Repeat with the remaining tortillas and fillings.

Transfer to a wire cooling rack as the the quesadillas are done and immediately sprinkle the taco shells with a pinch of flaky sea salt while they are still hot. Combine the sour cream and chili sauce and serve as a dipping sauce or place a dollop on each taco, and then top the tacos with cilantro, sliced serranos, and a squeeze of lime.

PRO TIP

Lightly brushing one side of the tortillas with the oil before placing them in a nonstick pan helps get them crispy without burning them.

My mom did not have the opportunity to graduate high school or go to college, but when she is in the kitchen, her confidence, mastery, and joy are unmatched.

WEEKEND PROJECTS

I grew up in a household of seventeen people, all under one roof! In the mid-1980s, my grandfather and all eight of his siblings came to the US, and in order to support one another in a new country and new way of life, they moved to the same community around Philadelphia. After this first group of families settled, they then hosted more of their extended families coming from India, until they too could get themselves established. Each family would pay it forward and host another group of relatives. This went on for years. My own family must have hosted relatives well into my early twenties.

It sounds chaotic thinking about it now, but as kids, we loved it. There was always someone to play, or fight, with, so we were never bored. Of course, this all meant that we had to make a lot of sacrifices, so while we didn't have much extra money for vacations, we always looked forward to the weekend, as it was the time we dedicated to building our little community, and it always revolved around food.

Cooking, hosting friends and family, and feeding people has always been a major part of our culture, and given the upbringing I had, it has become second nature to me.

The recipes in this chapter are perfect for weekends when you have the extra time to put into meals, especially when you're inviting people over for a game day or birthday celebration, or having a date night, or most any other occasion. I like to start with a big spread of apps and drinks (see pages 225–249), because I feel it's the most fun and filled with variety. A heartier spread of small bites also allows me to keep my dinner course simple, like an already prepared dish that's just waiting to hit the oven. The main course dinners in this chapter are one-pot/pan meals that are filling and easy to serve to a crowd. If you aren't doing apps, then by all means, add sides and/or a salad to create a more balanced spread.

And while these weekend projects do require more time and attention, the tradeoff is that they're designed to be prepared before guests arrive. None will go soggy or be overcooked. The filling for Spinach-Artichoke Lasagna Roll-Ups (page 143) can be made two days ahead, and the gravy for Chicken Makhni (page 153), the sauces for Mom's Falafel (page 146), and others can be made in advance to cut down on the work day of. These are also great dishes to take to a potluck, as they can be baked right before you go or once you arrive. Plus, they go well with almost anything else being served.

VEGETABLE ENCHILADAS

with POBLANO CREAM SAUCE

Serves 8

For the filling

3	tablespoons canola oil, plus more as needed
1	teaspoon cumin seeds
2	jalapeño chiles, diced
2	onions, sliced
1	red bell pepper, sliced
1	green bell pepper, sliced
2	tablespoons garlic, finely minced
2	(15-ounce/430 g) cans black beans, drained and rinsed
1	cup (145 g) frozen corn kernels, thawed, drained, and patted dry
4	tablespoons (35 g) taco seasoning
2	teaspoons red chili powder
2	teaspoons ground cumin
1	teaspoon salt
¼	teaspoon freshly ground black pepper
2	cups tightly packed (60 g) spinach leaves, roughly chopped
1	cup (55 g) sliced green onions
½	cup (20 g) finely chopped fresh cilantro
	A few dashes sriracha sauce (or your favorite hot sauce; optional)

When I first got married and started hosting dinners at our home, this was the dish I would make when having friends or family over. It has been a crowd favorite for years, and I hope it garners the same amount of praise from your loved ones as it has for me. Roasting the peppers, blending the sauce, and then assembling the enchiladas isn't something I'd want to do on a weeknight, but it's absolutely perfect for larger dinners and parties. Like all the recipes in this chapter, prepping is key; you can make the filling a day ahead and keep it refrigerated—and you can assemble the enchiladas in a baking dish and then just add the sauce and bake when you're ready to serve. This recipe makes double the sauce that you'll need, but it freezes beautifully (you can also freeze the entire dish). Try the extra sauce with Poblano Nachos with Chorizo (page 242), or toss it with some shredded rotisserie chicken as a delicious filling for taquitos!

MAKE THE FILLING: Heat the oil in a large skillet over medium-high heat, add the cumin seeds and jalapeños and stir for 30 seconds, until sizzling. Add the onions and red and green bell peppers, and cook for 5 to 7 minutes, until softened. Add the garlic, beans, and corn and continue to stir until the garlic is fragrant, 1 to 2 minutes. Add the taco seasoning, chili powder, cumin, salt, and pepper. Cook for 3 to 4 minutes, then add the spinach, green onions, and cilantro. Turn the heat off and stir in the hot sauce, if desired. Set aside until ready to assemble the enchiladas.

MAKE THE SAUCE: Set the broiler on high, and broil the poblanos on a baking sheet for 4 to 6 minutes on each side, until evenly charred and black on all sides.

Transfer the charred poblanos to a bowl and cover tightly for about 5 minutes. Once the skins have steamed and loosened, peel the charred skin, then cut the peppers open, remove the seeds and stems, and discard. Roughly chop the peppers and set aside.

continues

For the sauce

- 6 poblano chiles
- 3 tablespoons unsalted butter
- 2 tablespoons minced garlic
- 3 tablespoons all-purpose flour
- 2 cups (480 ml) vegetable broth
- 1¼ cups (300 ml) sour cream
- 2 cups (80 g) roughly chopped fresh cilantro (leaves and tender stems)
- 1 (4½-ounce/130 g) can diced green chiles
- 1 tablespoon ground cumin
  Salt
- ¼ cup (25 g) grated queso fresco or Pecorino Romano cheese

- 12 (10-inch/25 cm) flour tortillas
- 4 cups (455 g) shredded Mexican cheese blend or Monterey Jack cheese
  Pico de gallo, for garnish
  Queso fresco, for garnish

In a dutch oven or heavy-bottomed pot, heat the butter and garlic over medium heat and whisk in the flour until the roux has a nutty fragrance and is golden in color, 2 to 3 minutes.

Slowly whisk in the broth until the mixture is thick and bubbly. Next, add the sour cream, charred poblano peppers, cilantro, green chiles, cumin, and salt. Stir until smooth and all the ingredients are incorporated. Remove the pot from the heat. Using an electric hand blender (or a blender and carefully working in batches), blend the sauce until it is smooth and creamy. Stir the queso fresco into the sauce.

To assemble the enchiladas, preheat the oven to 375°F (190°C). Lightly oil two 9 by 13–inch (23 by 33 cm) baking dishes.

Pour about ¼ cup (60 ml) of the sauce on the bottom of the baking dish. Place a tortilla on a cutting board or the counter and add a generous cup or so of the filling. Spread the filling around the tortilla, top with a large handful of the cheese, and roll up tightly.

Heat 1 tablespoon oil in a large nonstick skillet over medium-high heat. Add the rolled enchiladas and cook on both sides until golden. Repeat with the remaining tortillas, using more oil as needed.

Place all of the enchiladas in the prepared baking dish and pour half of the sauce generously over the top. Freeze or use the rest of the sauce for another recipe.

Bake the enchiladas for 15 minutes or until hot and bubbly. Garnish with pico de gallo and queso fresco.

Spinach-Artichoke
LASAGNA ROLL-UPS

Makes 14 roll-ups; serves 6 to 8

For the pesto

1 cup loosely packed (30 g) spinach or any leafy green, such as kale or arugula

1 cup (40 g) fresh basil leaves

⅓ cup (30 g) grated Pecorino Romano cheese

1 cup (100 g) walnuts

Extra-virgin olive oil

2 cloves garlic, peeled

1 teaspoon crushed red pepper

½ teaspoon salt

Freshly ground black pepper

14 dried lasagna noodles (not instant cook)

For the filling

Extra-virgin olive oil

1 large yellow onion, finely chopped

1½ pounds (680 g) baby bella mushrooms, roughly chopped

1 teaspoon salt

1 (13.75-ounce/240 g) can artichoke hearts, drained, rinsed, and diced

1 (10-ounce/280 g) package frozen chopped spinach, thawed and squeezed dry

2 tablespoons minced garlic

2 teaspoons Italian seasoning

1½ teaspoons crushed red pepper, plus more for garnish

2½ cups (275 g) shredded mozzarella cheese

1 cup (245 g) ricotta cheese

¼ cup (13 g) chopped fresh parsley, plus more for garnish

This dish is rich, creamy, and super delicious. I love that it's one where you can make it all ahead of time and freeze it, then just pop it in the oven before serving. While I make my own pesto here, no one's judging you if you want to pick up your favorite store-bought version instead. To tackle this recipe, I suggest a battle plan of making (or buying!) the pesto first, then cooking the noodles, and then proceeding with the rest of the recipe.

MAKE THE PESTO: Combine the spinach, basil, Pecorino Romano, walnuts, ½ cup (120 ml) oil, the garlic, crushed red pepper, salt, and pepper in a food processor and pulse until all ingredients are smooth.

Lightly oil a half sheet pan. Cook the lasagna noodles in a large pot of salted boiling water for 8 minutes and drain. Using tongs, as the noodles will be very hot, arrange one layer of noodles flat on the sheet pan and lightly brush the noodles with oil to prevent them from sticking. Continue layering the noodles (or you can use wax or parchment paper between the layers) and cover with parchment or foil to keep them warm while you prepare the filling.

MAKE THE FILLING: Preheat the oven to 375°F (190°C). Lightly oil a 9 by 13–inch (23 by 33 cm) baking pan.

In a large skillet with high sides or a dutch oven, heat 2 tablespoons oil over medium-high. Add the onion and cook for about 3 minutes, until translucent. Add the mushrooms and salt and cook for 3 to 4 minutes, stirring often, until the mushrooms begin to cook down and release their liquid.

Reduce the heat to medium-low, add the artichoke hearts, spinach, garlic, Italian seasoning, and crushed red pepper and continue to cook for 2 to 3 minutes longer, or until the water has evaporated and the garlic is fragrant.

Transfer the mixture to a large bowl, and once the mixture has cooled, add 2 cups (220 g) of the mozzarella and the ricotta and half of the chopped parsley and stir until well combined.

continues

MAKE THE SAUCE: In a small pot over medium-low, heat the broth and the heavy cream with the bay leaf. (Alternatively, combine in a microwave-safe bowl and pop in the microwave for about 1 minute.) Set aside.

Melt the butter in a heavy-bottomed pot or dutch oven over medium heat, then whisk in the flour, stirring constantly, until the flour is golden in color and has a nutty aroma. Lower the heat and continue to whisk, slowly adding ½ cup (120 ml) of the vegetable broth mixture at a time, stirring constantly after each addition, until all of the liquid had been absorbed, creating a rich white sauce. This can take up to 10 minutes. Next, add the cheese and 1 cup (120 ml) of the pesto, and taste for salt (if your broth is very salty you may not need to add any) and black pepper and stir until well combined.

Pour 1 cup (240 ml) of the sauce into the bottom of the prepared baking pan. To assemble the roll-ups, spread a generous ¼ cup (60 ml) of the vegetable filling on each lasagna sheet and firmly roll them up. Place each roll in the pan with the seam side down. You should be able to fit three rolls across the short side of the pan.

Pour the remaining sauce evenly over the roll-ups. Cover with foil and bake for about 30 minutes, until golden and bubbly. Turn on the broiler, sprinkle the remaining ½ cup (55 g) mozzarella cheese over the top, and carefully brown the cheese under the broiler, 1 to 2 minutes.

Remove from the oven and let the roll-ups set for 5 minutes. Garnish with additional chopped parsley and crushed red pepper. Serve immediately.

For the sauce

- 3 cups (720 ml) vegetable broth
- 1 cup (240 ml) heavy cream
- 1 bay leaf
- 3 tablespoons unsalted butter
- 3 tablespoons all-purpose flour
- ⅓ cup (30 g) grated Parmigiano-Reggiano cheese

  Salt and freshly ground black pepper

PRO TIP

When it comes to cooking lasagna noodles, a trick I swear by is to place the cooked noodles on lightly oiled sheet pans and lightly oil each noodle; lay them flat, and cover to keep warm and pliable as you finish the recipe.

MOM'S FALAFEL

Serves 4

For the white sauce

- 2 tablespoons toasted sesame seeds
- 2 cups (480 ml) mayonnaise
- ½ cup (120 ml) whole-milk plain yogurt
- 2 tablespoons sriracha sauce
- 1 teaspoon sugar
- 1½ teaspoons garlic powder
- ½ teaspoon freshly ground black pepper
- 4 cloves garlic, grated
- ½ teaspoon red chili powder
- ½ teaspoon salt, plus more if needed
- 1 tablespoon finely chopped fresh cilantro
- 1 tablespoon finely chopped fresh parsley

For the red sauce

- 12 dried red chiles, soaked in hot water for at least 3 hours
- 3 red bell peppers, preferably dark red, roughly chopped
- 1½ teaspoons cumin seeds
- 6 cloves garlic, peeled
- 1½ teaspoons salt, plus more if needed

If there is one dish that my entire family unanimously agrees is the best thing my mom makes, it's these falafel. Everybody from my grandmother to my nieces and nephews is obsessed with them—and for good reason! Let's start with the white sauce—it's sweeter than a traditional tahini yogurt situation, but it's garlicky, and the fresh sesame seeds really stand out. The red sauce, which can be lethal depending on the heat of your dried red chiles, can be treated like a hot sauce, but it's almost better than a hot sauce because instead of just a vinegary heat, it adds a delicious flavor and brightness to the entire dish. The prep for the falafel is best split up over a few days and the sauces keep well for a few days, so get those out of the way. Store them in squeeze bottles because I promise when you get halfway through your pita and falafel sandwich, you're going to want to squeeze on more sauce! Instead of serving these in a traditional pita pocket, you can also tear up the pita into chunks and toss this together like a salad.

MAKE THE WHITE SAUCE: Using a mortar and pestle, small spice or coffee grinder, or a rolling pin on a cutting board, grind the sesame seeds to a paste. In a medium bowl, combine the crushed sesame seeds with the mayonnaise, yogurt, sriracha, sugar, garlic powder, black pepper, garlic, chili powder, salt, cilantro, and parsley. Stir well and taste for seasoning and adjust as needed. Refrigerate until ready to use.

MAKE THE RED SAUCE: Strain the red chiles and add them to a blender with the bell peppers, cumin seeds, garlic, and salt. Blend on high until completely smooth. Taste and adjust the salt as needed. Refrigerate until ready to use.

MAKE THE FALAFEL: Line a sheet pan with paper towels.

In a colander, drain the soaked masoor dal well and transfer to a food processor with the serranos and garlic. Pulse until you have a coarse mixture, about 1 minute. Transfer to a bowl and set aside until ready to fry.

When ready to fry, using your hands, evenly incorporate the sesame seeds and salt into the dal. As you mix the batter with your hands (make sure you really get in there!), the salt will begin to release liquid and the mixture will become fluffier.

Pour canola oil into a wide-bottomed pot or dutch oven until it comes 2 inches (5 cm) up the side of the pot. Heat the oil over medium-high heat. Use a frying or candy thermometer to check the temperature of the oil; it should range from 350°F to 375°F (175°C to 190°F). If you don't have a thermometer, you can test the oil by dropping a small pinch of batter into the oil; if it instantly rises to the top and the oil is sizzling, the oil is ready.

Use a cookie scoop to loosely scoop the batter into roughly 1-inch (2.5 cm) balls and drop them into the oil. You may have to lightly pack the balls with your hands if the mixture is too loose. Test one or two first—they may cook in 30 seconds to 1 minute. Taste for salt and seasoning and adjust the batter as needed. Continue to add the balls to the oil, but do not overcrowd; leave enough space so you can turn the balls with a slotted spoon so that they brown evenly and do not stick together. A full batch will take about 1½ minutes to fry. You may need to lower or raise the heat as you cook; a thermometer is very helpful to gauge proper temperature.

Carefully remove the falafel with a large slotted spoon or spider and place onto the prepared sheet tray to drain. Repeat until you've used up all the batter. You can keep the falafel warm in a 200°F (90°C) oven until ready to serve.

To assemble, warm the pitas in the microwave for about 10 seconds. Spread white sauce and a tiny bit of red sauce inside the warm pitas, add lettuce, cucumbers, and 3 to 4 falafel balls, gently smashed, and top with more white sauce and red sauce, tomatoes, and onion. Serve warm or at room temperature.

For the falafel

- 2 cups (400 g) whole masoor dal, soaked overnight in hot water
- 15 to 20 serrano chiles, roughly chopped
- 14 cloves garlic, peeled and roughly chopped
- 1 tablespoon sesame seeds
- 1 tablespoon salt, plus more if needed
  Canola oil, for frying

- 8 pita pockets (see Note)
- 2 cups (110 g) chopped romaine lettuce
- 3 Persian cucumbers, chopped small
- 3 plum tomatoes, seeds removed, small diced
- 1 large red onion, small diced

PRO TIP

Don't be confused with the variety of masoor dal that is red in color; whole masoor dal is olive green to brownish in color and will yield a very different texture!

NOTE

I like the sliced pita pocket thins from the bread aisle—they're already cut perfectly in half. If using whole pitas, cut off the top one-fourth of the pita and fill.

MOM'S FALAFEL, PAGE 146

Warning: Falafel will mysteriously disappear during the assembly process. Also, how cute is my mama?!

LAMB KHEEMA– STUFFED PEPPERS

Serves 6

For the poblano peppers

- 6 poblano chiles (8 if they are small)
- 2 tablespoons canola oil
- ¼ teaspoon salt

For the sauce

- 2 tablespoons unsalted butter
- 2 tablespoons all-purpose flour
- 1 teaspoon grated garlic
- 1½ cups (360 ml) chicken broth, warmed in the microwave for about 40 seconds
- 1 cup (240 ml) heavy cream, warmed in the microwave for about 40 seconds
- 1 teaspoon Cajun seasoning
- ⅛ teaspoon garam masala
- ¼ teaspoon Italian seasoning
   Freshly ground black pepper
- 1 cup (100 g) shredded Pecorino Romano cheese

Spicy ground lamb is tossed with jeera rice and decadent béchamel, then tucked into perfectly blistered peppers to make an ideal meal or side. These stuffed peppers are delicious, hearty, and you won't miss the carbs! When I've served a ton of heavy appetizers and want some solid protein for dinner that still feels like a well-rounded meal, these are what I serve: They are satisfying but don't make you feel like you need to undo the button on your pants. You can also prep them completely and take them to a potluck as a side dish—just pop in the oven and bake when you get there. The lamb kheema is also great to use all week in salads, tacos, breakfast burritos, and more.

Preheat the oven to 400°F (205°C).

MAKE THE POBLANO PEPPERS: Cut them in half lengthwise and remove the stem and inner part of the pepper so it is hollow.

Lightly oil both sides of the peppers and sprinkle with salt. Place them cut side down on a baking sheet lined with aluminum foil and bake until they have softened and the outsides are lightly browned, 15 to 20 minutes, turning them midway through. Remove the tray and carefully close up the foil into a sealed package so they continue to steam as you prepare the filling and sauce.

MAKE THE SAUCE: In a medium saucepan over medium heat, melt the butter until it is foaming. Add the flour and garlic and stir until the flour becomes slightly golden in color and has a nutty aroma, 1 to 2 minutes. Reduce the heat slightly, and slowly pour in the broth in small increments, whisking constantly after each addition. Whisk in the cream slowly and bring to a very low simmer. Add the Cajun seasoning, garam masala, Italian seasoning, and black pepper. Stir to combine and then remove from the heat and stir in the Pecorino Romano. Set aside.

continues

For the lamb kheema

- 2 tablespoons ghee
- 2 bay leaves
- 5 peppercorns
- 1 star anise
- 1 teaspoon cumin seeds
- 3 Thai green chiles, finely diced
- 1 large onion, finely diced
- 1 teaspoon salt
- 2 tablespoons tomato paste
- ½ teaspoon ground turmeric
- 2 teaspoons ground cumin
- 1 teaspoon garam masala
- 1½ teaspoons ground coriander
- 2 tablespoons garlic
- 1 tablespoon grated fresh ginger
- 1 pound (455 g) ground lamb
- 1 cup (180 g) Jeera Rice (page 181) or cooked white rice
- ¼ cup (10 g) finely chopped fresh cilantro, plus more for garnish
- ⅓ cup (50 g) peas

- 1 cup (110 g) store-bought shredded mozzarella cheese

MAKE THE LAMB KHEEMA: Set a large, high-sided cooking pan or dutch oven over medium-high heat and add the ghee. Once it is shimmering, add the bay leaves, peppercorns, star anise, and cumin seeds and cook for about 15 seconds.

Add the green chiles, quickly stir, and add the onion and salt. Reduce the heat slightly and cook, stirring occasionally, until golden, 6 to 8 minutes.

Add the tomato paste, stir, and cook for 2 minutes. Add the turmeric, cumin, garam masala, coriander, garlic, and ginger and cook for another 2 minutes. Add the ground lamb and use a wooden spatula to break it up into small pieces. Cook until no longer pink, and the meat is cooked through.

Add ¾ cup (180 ml) water, stir, cover, and cook for about 5 minutes. Gently fold in the jeera rice, taking care not to mash it. Gently stir in the cilantro and peas.

To assemble, place 2 cups (480 ml) of the sauce on the bottom of a 9 by 13–inch (23 by 33 cm) baking dish and arrange the hollow roasted peppers on top, tucking them together, so they are snug and stay put. Use a spoon to carefully fill each of the peppers with the lamb kheema. If your peppers are small, cover the surface as best you can, and then simply layer the lamb over the entire surface of the baking dish.

Pour the remainder of the sauce on top of all the peppers, add the mozzarella, cover with foil, and bake for about 20 minutes. Remove the foil, set the oven to broil on low, and broil for 2 to 3 minutes, until the cheese is slightly golden. Serve immediately.

CHICKEN MAKHNI

Serves 6

For the chicken

- 2 tablespoons canola oil
- 1 tablespoon fresh lemon juice
- 2 tablespoons whole-milk plain yogurt
- 2 teaspoons garlic powder
- 2 teaspoons garam masala
- 2 teaspoons red chili powder
- 2 teaspoons ground cumin
- 2 teaspoons ground coriander
- 1 teaspoon onion powder
- 1 tablespoon grated garlic
- 2 teaspoons peeled and grated fresh ginger
- ½ teaspoon salt
- 1½ pounds (680 g) boneless, skinless chicken breasts
- ½ medium onion, cut into ½-inch (12 mm) dice
- ½ green bell pepper, cut into ½-inch (12 mm) dice

For the makhni (gravy)

- 2 tablespoons canola oil
- 1 teaspoon cumin seeds
- 1 star anise
- 2 bay leaves
- 1 (1-inch/2.5 cm) piece cinnamon stick
- 2 cardamom pods
- 4 dried red chiles
- 5 black peppercorns
- ½ small onion, chopped
- 1 (1-inch/2.5 cm) piece fresh ginger, roughly chopped
- 2 Thai green chiles, finely chopped
- 3 plum tomatoes, roughly chopped

Butter chicken, chicken makhni, chicken tikka masala—you've seen these on menus across the world. They're the quintessential dishes that come to mind when people think of "Indian food." They're creamy, tomato-based, laden with butter, and usually reliably delicious go-to options at most Indian restaurants. I love making this dish during the holidays, because after all the appetizers and cocktails and socializing, it's nice to offer something satisfying. I serve it with naan, Chaat Onions (page 260), Jeera Rice (page 181), Classic Raita (page 259), and a hefty side of papad, sometimes called pappadum, which are thin crackers that can be found in South Asian markets or online. You buy them dried, then throw them in the microwave, and they add crunch and spice to your dish.

MAKE THE CHICKEN: In a large bowl, combine the oil, lemon juice, yogurt, garlic powder, garam masala, chili powder, cumin, coriander, onion powder, garlic, ginger, and salt. Add the chicken and with your hands or a spatula, rub the marinade all over the chicken until well coated. Add the onion and bell pepper and stir to coat them evenly with the marinade. Cover the chicken and refrigerate for at least 3 hours or overnight.

Preheat the oven to 375°F (190°C). Line a baking sheet with foil.

Place the chicken, onion, bell pepper, and marinade on the prepared sheet pan and bake for 30 minutes, turning the breasts halfway through. Set aside for 10 minutes to cool. Transfer the chicken to a cutting board, cut into small, bite-size cubes, and return it to the pan.

MAKE THE MAKHNI (GRAVY): Add the oil to a large skillet with high sides or a large dutch oven and heat over medium. Once the oil is shimmering, add the cumin seeds, star anise, bay leaves, cinnamon stick, cardamom, dried red chiles, and peppercorns. Stir for about 30 seconds, until the spices become fragrant, taking care not to burn the chiles.

Reduce the heat slightly and add the onion, ginger, and green chiles and cook for about 6 minutes, stirring frequently, until the onion is golden brown around the edges. Add the tomatoes and cook until they are jammy and broken down, about 5 minutes, using the back of a spatula to mash the tomatoes as they cook.

continues

2	tablespoons tomato paste
1	tablespoon grated garlic
1½	teaspoons salt
1	teaspoon red chili powder
½	cup (1 stick/115 g) unsalted butter
¼	cup (45 g) kasoori methi (fenugreek)
1	tablespoon honey
¼	teaspoon garam masala
1½	cups (360 ml) heavy cream
¼	cup (10 g) finely chopped fresh cilantro, for garnish

PRO TIP

Make light work of this recipe by marinating the chicken in the fridge the night before. You can also make the gravy ahead and cook and combine it with the chicken before serving, or make the gravy as the chicken bakes.

Carefully use a spoon to remove the star anise, bay leaves, and cinnamon stick. Add the tomato paste, garlic, 1 cup (240 ml) water, salt, and chili powder and stir well to combine; reduce the heat to medium-low and cover. Simmer for 20 minutes, stirring occasionally.

Carefully transfer the mixture, including the cardamom and peppercorns, to a blender, in batches if necessary, and blend on high until completely smooth and uniform.

Wipe the pan and set it over medium-low and add the butter. Once melted, carefully add the tomato mixture from the blender and stir to combine. Place the kasoori methi in your hands and rub your palms together to crush it finely; add to the gravy. Add the honey, garam masala, and heavy cream and stir well to combine.

Add the cubed chicken, along with the onion, bell pepper, and the juices from the baking pan. Adjust for salt and pepper as needed. Garnish with chopped cilantro. Serve immediately.

PANEER MAKHNI

Serves 6

2 tablespoons canola oil

1 teaspoon cumin seeds

½ onion, dices

½ green bell pepper, diced

½ red bell pepper, diced

1 tablespoon minced garlic

2 teaspoons grated ginger

2 teaspoons ground cumin

2 teaspoons ground coriander

1 teaspoon red chili powder

1 teaspoon garam masala

½ teaspoon salt

1 pound (455 g) paneer, diced

2 teaspoons finely chopped fresh cilantro

Makhni (gravy; see page 153), warmed over medium-low heat

I love having a good, classic recipe up my sleeve, and this one for paneer makhni is one I find myself making again and again. It's creamy, easy to completely prepare ahead of time, and not fussy to serve, either. You can add in different veggies along with the paneer based on your preference or keep it simple, your choice! This makhni sauce is also incredibly versatile (see the chicken version on page 153), so have fun with it!

Heat the oil in a large cooking pan over medium-high heat. Add the cumin seeds. Once they begin to sizzle, add the onion and green and red peppers. Cook for about 5 minutes, or until they are softened, stirring frequently and lowering the heat if necessary.

Lower the heat to medium and add the garlic and ginger. Cook for about 2 minutes, stirring frequently, until fragrant. Add the cumin, coriander, chili powder, garam masala, and salt and cook for an additional 2 minutes. Add ¼ cup (60 ml) water and stir to create a paste. Add the paneer and cilantro. Cook for 3 to 4 minutes, stirring occasionally, until the paneer is soft and coated in the spices. You may need to add a few more tablespoons water, to loosen the spices. You don't want a broth, but you don't want the spices to burn, either.

Remove from the heat and add the paneer to the warmed makhni. Serve immediately.

KOFTA SUBS

Serves 4

For the kofta

- 2 large potatoes, peeled and cut into large chunks
- 1 carrot, peeled and grated
- 7 ounces (200 g) paneer, grated
- 2 Thai green chiles, finely chopped
- 1½ teaspoons peeled and grated fresh ginger
- 6 large cloves garlic, grated
- 1½ teaspoons salt
- 3 tablespoons cornstarch
- Canola oil

For the rolls

- 4 (6-inch/15 cm) hoagie rolls, cut three-fourths of the way through
- ¾ cup (1½ sticks/170 g) unsalted butter, softened
- ¼ teaspoon salt
- 2 teaspoons dried oregano
- 1 teaspoon crushed red pepper
- 4 cloves garlic, grated

For assembly

- 3 cups (720 ml) prepared marinara sauce, warmed (I love Rao's Arrabbiata)
- 4 to 8 slices white American cheese
- ⅓ cup (80 g) chopped pickled jalapeño chiles and their juice
- 3 jalapeño chiles, chopped
- 3 tablespoons chopped fresh cilantro
- 2 tablespoons grated Pecorino Romano cheese

My mom made malai kofta all the time when I was growing up, and while I never ate the entire dish as it was meant to be eaten, with the gravy and naan and rice and all that, I could not get enough of the fried kofta made from potatoes and paneer. So, before she dunked them into the gravy, much to her annoyance, my brother and I would steal a few of the kofta.

These kofta subs are kinda, sorta my take on a vegetarian Indian-inspired meatball sub, as they are served on a crusty hoagie roll topped with marinara and sliced cheese. This recipe falls under my "labor of love" category, but the kofta are highly unique, making them great to prepare for guests. We love making these during football season, as they are the perfect game-day dinner fare!

Preheat the oven to 375°F (190°C). Line a baking sheet with foil. Line another baking sheet with paper towels.

MAKE THE KOFTA: Place the potatoes in a small pot and add water to cover. Bring to a boil and cook until tender, about 20 minutes. Drain. Use a potato ricer or grate the potatoes on the large holes of a box grater into a large bowl. Add the carrot, paneer, green chiles, ginger, garlic, salt, and cornstarch, and with your hands, mix everything evenly and gently to form a "dough." Lightly oil your hands, then use them to roll the potato mixture into medium-size (about 1½ inches/4 cm in diameter) "meatballs." You will have 26 or so uniform kofta.

In a medium saucepan, add enough canola oil to come up 2 inches (5 cm) the sides of the pan. Heat over medium-high until the oil reaches 375°F (190°C) on a candy or deep-fry thermometer. Fry the kofta in batches for 2 to 3 minutes, until they are golden brown, then place them on the paper towel–lined baking sheet.

PREPARE THE ROLLS: Gently spread the rolls apart to open them, being careful not to break them, and place them split side up on the foil-lined baking sheet. If they seem very "bready," remove some of the interior bread.

In a small bowl, stir the butter, salt, oregano, crushed red pepper, and garlic until evenly combined. Spread about 2 teaspoons of the garlic butter onto both sides of each roll. Bake for about 5 minutes, or until the outer edges of the roll are slightly golden. Remove the rolls from the oven.

TO ASSEMBLE: Spread marinara sauce on both sides of each roll and top with 4 to 5 kofta. Place 1 to 2 slices of cheese over the kofta, and place the rolls back into the oven for 3 to 4 minutes to let the kofta and sauce warm up and the cheese melt. Meanwhile, in a small bowl, mix together the pickled jalapeños and their juice, fresh jalapeños, cilantro, and Pecorino Romano. Remove the subs from the oven and place them on a platter. Divide the jalapeño garnish evenly among the subs. Serve warm.

PATEL FAMILY RECIPES

I can just picture the sheer joy spreading across my mom's face as she flips through the pages of this chapter. All the foods she forced me to eat as a child and warned me I would miss as an adult are here, and I have to admit, she was right!

I take great pride and responsibility in sharing and documenting these heirloom recipes. They are as nostalgic as they are delicious, and I am so honored to share them with you.

The Patel family recipes don't need a trendy twist, no reinventing or reimagining; instead, they're meant to be enjoyed in their original and classic form. For example, my mom's ghee-laden dal fry, my go-to meal after a weekend of going out to eat and over-indulging, is made the same way it has been for generations. It's the way my grandmother taught my mother, and my mother taught me.

The thing I love about Indian food, and the recipes in this chapter, is that they are nutritious and wholesome. The truth is, now that my parents and in-laws are older, when they come to my house for dinner or lunch, they have less tolerance for processed or unfamiliar foods. I started running out of ideas of what to make, so I started leaning into more traditional dishes, ones that I knew would be satisfying but would also keep these family members feeling healthy. Many of the recipes use lentils, legumes (FYI, there will be a good deal of soaking things overnight, so keep this in mind), and vegetables, without much added dairy or gluten, so they work really well for anyone with dietary restrictions.

I also encourage you to take a moment and appreciate the combination of flavors that are important to Gujarati cuisine, such as sweet, spicy, and sour. Kala Chana Nu Shaak (page 179) and Bataka Poha (page 162) both call for sugar and lime to help achieve a balance of flavors that leaves you wanting more. While I've noted all of this in headnotes, feel free to adjust the seasonings in any of the recipes in this chapter, and throughout the book, to your taste and liking. Each family that makes these traditional recipes puts their own stamp on them. Now it's your turn to make them your own!

BATAKA POHA

Serves 4

For the poha

- 2 cups (140 g) thick poha (flattened rice; can be found in South Asian markets or online)
- ½ teaspoon red chili powder
- ½ teaspoon ground turmeric
- 2 teaspoons sugar
- 1½ tablespoons fresh lemon juice

For the potatoes

- 3 tablespoons canola oil
- 1 teaspoon mustard seeds
- 1½ teaspoons cumin seeds
- 2 Thai green chiles
- 10 curry leaves
- ¼ teaspoon hing (asafetida)
- 1 small onion, diced
- 1 teaspoon salt, plus more as needed
- 2 small potatoes, diced and soaked in water until ready to use
- 1 tomato, diced
- ¼ cup (10 g) chopped fresh cilantro (leaves and tender stems)
  Freshly ground black pepper

  Cilantro Chutney (page 193), for garnish

  Sev (Ratlami brand), for garnish

When I was growing up, breakfast in my house was the typical assortment of nastho (which in my household consisted of fried or roasted dry snacks—think savory and spicy cereals and trail mixes), accompanied by a cup of kadak (aka strong) chai. Rarely did we stray from this during the week, but bataka poha (made from flattened rice) was usually a constant on the weekend menu. On Sundays, when the whole house just wanted to sleep in and have a lazy morning, we'd skip the dry snacks and have a bowl of hot poha with our chai instead. It's lightly spiced, so not too overwhelming to have first thing in the morning, and if you're having it later in the day, it will definitely hold you over until dinner. This is also eaten many ways across India. You can top it with sev—fried, crunchy snacks made from a batter of chickpea flour and spices that are used as a topping on many dishes to add flavor and texture—and chutney, skip the tomatoes, or even make this with sweet potatoes. I love mine with an extra squeeze of lemon on top!

PREPARE THE POHA: Rinse the flattened rice in a bowl 5 or 6 times, until the water runs clear. Transfer the rinsed poha to a bowl and toss with the chili powder, turmeric, sugar, and lemon juice. Set aside.

PREPARE THE POTATOES: In a large skillet, heat the oil over medium-high heat and add the mustard seeds. When they begin to pop, add the cumin seeds, green chiles, curry leaves, and hing and quickly stir to combine.

Lower the heat to medium, add the onion and salt, and cook for 2 to 3 minutes, stirring occasionally. Drain the potatoes and add them to the pan, reduce the heat to medium-low, cover, and cook until the potatoes are fork-tender, 6 to 8 minutes, stirring occasionally to prevent sticking.

Once the potatoes are fork-tender, add the tomatoes and cook for 2 to 3 minutes, until the tomatoes are soft, stirring occasionally. Add the poha and cilantro, toss well to combine, and cook for an additional 2 to 3 minutes. Season with salt and pepper and serve hot with a dollop of cilantro chutney and a handful of sev.

CHILI ONION UTTAPAM

with COCONUT CILANTRO CHUTNEY

Serves 4 to 6

2½   cups (450 g) basmati rice

1   cup (140 g) urad dal

1   teaspoon salt

Canola oil, as needed

1   large red onion, diced

½   cup (20 g) finely chopped fresh cilantro

4   to 5 green Anaheim chiles, diced

¼   cup (60 g) achar masala

3   large tomatoes, diced, seeds removed

Coconut Cilantro Chutney (page 255)

This dish is a weekend go-to in our house, as well as one of Pinank's favorite meals, and this version that my MIL taught me is my favorite way to make it. Uttapam, popular in Southern India, is a thick, savory pancake that is often topped with an assortment of vegetables. A cousin to dosa, it's eaten with sambhar, a stew made from lentils, and a variety of chutneys. While uttapam batter can be a laborious process that involves soaking rice and dal, then blending it and letting it ferment, this recipe requires far less effort. You can play around with the toppings and use different veggies, but I love sticking to the classics, such as onions, chiles, and tomatoes. If you want to up the heat, swap the Anaheim chiles for ones with more heat, like serranos or Thai green chiles. I make this often without the sambhar; instead I'm sharing the recipe for my favorite Coconut Cilantro Chutney, which I eat with every bite! This makes a generous batch of uttapam batter, so freeze half for next time and just thaw it out before using by placing it in the fridge overnight. Making this will require a quick visit to the South Asian market or online for urad dal, achar masala, frozen coconut, chana dalia, and other ingredients, so plan ahead and don't take any shortcuts on this one. It's totally worth the effort!

Rinse the rice and urad dal 2 to 3 times, until the water runs clear. I find this easiest if you place the rice and beans in separate colanders with bowls underneath them; fill them with water, swish around, lift the colanders, drain, and repeat. Then soak them in separate bowls with enough water to cover them by a few inches for a minimum of 4 hours and up to 6 hours on the counter. You can loosely cover them with foil.

Drain the rice and urad dal completely and transfer to a blender. Add the salt and 2¼ cups (540 ml) water and blend on the highest speed until it is completely smooth, about 25 seconds. You may need to blend in batches, depending on your blender capacity. Transfer the batter to a bowl.

Heat a medium nonstick skillet over medium-high. Once the skillet is hot, coat with a thin layer of oil.

continues

Pour about ⅓ cup (75 ml) of the batter into the center of the skillet. It should naturally spread out into a disc. Use the flat underside of the measuring cup to spread the batter out to make it a little thinner. You should start to see some holes form (that's how you know it's thin enough). If for some reason it isn't thin enough, add a little water to the batter.

Immediately sprinkle the disc with some red onion, cilantro, green chiles, a generous sprinkle of achar masala, and tomatoes. Use a spatula to press the toppings down into the batter. Drizzle ½ teaspoon or so of oil along the outer edges of the uttapam, lifting your pan off the heat and moving it around to help the oil get to the edges evenly.

When the underside of the uttapam is slightly golden, carefully flip the uttapam and press it with your spatula. Cook for about 1 minute, allowing the toppings to slightly char. Use your spatula to lift the uttapam up and place it directly on a serving plate, topping side up. Serve with cilantro coconut chutney.

BHARELA RINGAN & BATAKA

Serves 4

For the spice blend

- ½ teaspoon ajwain seeds, crushed between your palms
- 1 tablespoon ground cumin
- 1 tablespoon ground coriander
- 2 teaspoons red chili powder
- 1 teaspoon garam masala
- 1½ teaspoons amchur powder
- 2½ teaspoons salt
- 2 tablespoons grated jaggery
- 1 teaspoon ground turmeric
- ¼ teaspoon hing (asafetida)
- ½ cup (70 g) raw peanuts
- 2 tablespoons sesame seeds

For the eggplant and potatoes

- 8 ounces (225 g) baby eggplants
- 10 baby creamer potatoes, peeled
- 3 tablespoons besan (chickpea flour)
- ¼ cup (60 ml) plus 2 tablespoons canola oil
- 4 cloves garlic, grated
- ½ cup (20 g) chopped fresh cilantro (leaves and tender stems)
- Salt, as needed

Okay, confession time: When I was a child, all the bribery in the world could not get me to eat stuffed potatoes and eggplant. It just always felt like "adult" food and, frankly, nothing I wanted any part of. Of course, life is full of curveballs, and let me tell you, I was absolutely blown away when I tried this dish for the first time as—*drumroll*—an adult. The stuffing, made from toasted sesame seeds and peanuts, is where the magic truly happens. It's sweet, spicy, nutty, and has a delicious grainy texture that stands up well to the fork-tender potatoes and eggplant. While this can be part of a traditional meal and eaten with paratha or rice, I love it on its own, with a little smear of Cilantro Jalapeño Sauce (page 252). A little unconventional but SO good. There will be leftover stuffing that can be refrigerated and used to stuff other vegetables, such as shishito peppers, jalapeños, or even baby onions.

MAKE THE SPICE BLEND: Add the ajwain seeds, cumin, coriander, chili powder, garam masala, amchur powder, salt, jaggery, turmeric, and hing to a small bowl and mix to combine.

In a spice grinder or mini food processor, blend the peanuts and sesame seeds until coarsely ground, resembling the texture of breadcrumbs.

MAKE THE EGGPLANT AND POTATOES: Remove the caps from the eggplants and cut them crosswise about three-fourths of the way through, leaving the bottom one-fourth of the eggplant intact to be stuffed. Peel the potatoes and cut in the same manner.

Heat a medium saucepan over medium and add the besan. Cook for about 3 minutes, until it is nutty and fragrant, stirring constantly so the flour doesn't brown too quickly. Add the peanut and sesame seed mixture and continue to cook for an additional 2 minutes, until everything is toasty and slightly golden. Remove the pan from the heat and add the contents to the spice blend.

continues

Allow the mixture to cool slightly, then add 2 tablespoons of the oil, the garlic, and cilantro to the spice mixture and mix well with your fingers to blend everything together so it is uniform and there are no big clumps. Stuff about 1 generous tablespoon of the filling into each eggplant and potato, being careful not to split them open. (If they do split, press them back together.)

In a 10-inch (25 cm) cooking pan with tall sides, heat the remaining ¼ cup (60 ml) oil over medium-high. Place the potatoes and eggplants in the pan in a single layer. Carefully pour ½ cup (120 ml) water into the pan (it will steam and sizzle a little), and cover with a tight-fitting lid. Reduce the heat slightly to medium and cook for 20 to 30 minutes, turning the eggplants and potatoes every 5 minutes or so, so they brown evenly. If the stuffing spills during turning and is stuck to the bottom of the pan, add about another ¼ cup (60 ml) water while cooking to keep it from burning.

The eggplant cooks faster than the potatoes, so once you can easily pierce the potatoes with a knife, both the eggplant and potatoes are done. Remove from the heat. Adjust salt, if needed, and serve.

My mother-in-law with Shaan and me!

MIL'S
SEV USSAL

Serves 4

1⅓ cups (265 g) white vatana (white pigeon peas)

1 teaspoon salt

3 tablespoons oil

1½ teaspoons cumin seeds

3 Thai green chiles, finely chopped

1 large red onion, diced

1½ tablespoons minced garlic

1 tablespoon peeled and grated fresh ginger

2 tomatoes, diced

1 tablespoon tomato paste

¼ teaspoon ground turmeric

2 teaspoons red chili powder

1 teaspoon ground coriander

1 teaspoon ground cumin

2½ teaspoons salt, plus more if needed

½ teaspoon garam masala

¼ cup (10 g) finely chopped fresh cilantro (leaves and tender stems)

Handfuls of sev

Cilantro Chutney (page 193)

Plain yogurt (optional)

PRO TIP

This is one of those dishes that tastes better as the day goes on and the flavors build, so make it and then let it sit in the pot for a few hours until ready to serve! To keep its brothy consistency, when reheating this, make sure it is covered so the liquid doesn't evaporate.

Sev ussal is spicy, brothy soup, and for me it provides the type of comfort one gets from a big bowl of chicken noodle soup. Plus, I submerge in mine so much sev (see headnote, page 162)—the way someone drowns in their soup crackers or tortilla strips—that you can barely tell what I am eating. When I was pregnant with Sahil, I had my MIL make me huge batches of sev ussal for the upcoming week. I've had many versions of sev ussal over the years, but I love my MIL's for how "soupy" it is, and in the words of Shaan, "cozy cozy." My family loves it with a big spoonful of Cilantro Chutney and a dollop of yogurt to help cool down the spice. Adjust the spice level to your liking by reducing or increasing the amount of red chili powder and Thai green chiles. Sev come in different sizes and thickness; for saucy and soup dishes like this one, I like a type called "ratlami" because they really hold up to all the sauciness.

Soak the white vatana overnight in a medium bowl with 2 inches (5 cm) of water covering them. In the morning, rinse the vatana a couple of times and put the drained vatana into an Instant Pot with 4 cups (960 ml) water and the salt. Set the mode to high pressure, cook for 30 minutes, and then quick release the pressure. Set aside.

Heat the oil in a dutch oven or large pot over medium-high heat. Add the cumin seeds and heat until they begin to sizzle. Add the green chiles and stir for 10 seconds. Add the red onion, reduce the heat to medium-low, and cook until the onion begins to turn golden brown around the edges, 8 to 10 minutes, stirring often.

Add the garlic, ginger, tomatoes, tomato paste, turmeric, chili powder, coriander, cumin, and salt and cook for 5 to 6 minutes, stirring often and using the back of the spatula to mash down the tomatoes, so they're completely broken down.

Add the white vatana, along with all of the cooking liquid plus 2 cups (480 ml) water, stir well, and increase the heat to bring the mixture to a boil. Reduce the heat to a simmer, cover, and cook for 10 minutes. Add the garam masala and cilantro, and additional salt if needed. Serve hot with a handful of sev on top and a dollop of cilantro chutney and yogurt.

MASOOR DAL PUDLA

Serves 4

1½   cups (270 g) whole masoor dal

12   cloves garlic

2½   teaspoons salt

6   serrano chiles, roughly chopped

2   tablespoons sesame seeds

    Canola oil

I can quite literally think of a million ways to make pudla! These thin, savory crepes are made simply from lentils and not a ton of other ingredients, which allows for the flavor of the masoor dal to fully come through. When I introduced solid foods to six-month-old Shaan, I would make him different varieties of pudla every few days because they were nutritious, involved minimal ingredients, and the batter was easy to make in big batches and freeze. If you make these for kids, you can add a handful of spinach into the batter and reduce the garlic and green chiles based on their preferences. These are also gluten-free, dairy-free, and obviously delicious!

Soak the masoor dal overnight in water to cover by 2 inches (5 cm).

Drain and rinse the masoor and place in a food processor, along with the garlic, salt, and serranos, and process until completely smooth, about 1 minute, stopping to scrape down the sides to evenly blend.

Empty into a bowl, add the sesame seeds and 1¼ cups (300 ml) water and mix until everything is well combined.

Heat a large nonstick skillet over medium heat and drizzle with oil, then wipe any excess oil out of the pan with a paper towel. Once the skillet is hot, add about ⅓ cup (75 ml) batter to the center of the skillet and use the flat bottom of the measuring cup or back of a large serving spoon to spread the batter into a circle that is even in thickness and about 8 inches (20 cm) across. Try to get them as thin as you can without the batter leaving any open holes; this may take some practice, and if yours are thicker that's okay, too. Once the batter begins to cook, drizzle half a teaspoon of oil along the outer edges of the pudla, and let it heat for a few seconds. Then, use a spatula to lift the outer edges of the pudla, tilt the pan so some of the oil gathers at the center of the pan, and then flip the pudla and cook the other side for 20 to 30 seconds, until golden brown. Remove from the heat and serve hot.

CLASSIC PARATHA

Makes 1 dozen paratha

3   cups (360 g) whole-wheat atta flour, plus ½ cup (60 g) for dusting

2   teaspoons salt

1   teaspoon ajwain seeds

3   tablespoons canola oil, plus more for cooking

⅓   cup (75 ml) ghee, for cooking

PRO TIP

A few things to note before making this recipe—there are a ton of different "atta" or whole-wheat flour brands when you peruse the aisle at your local South Asian market or online. Different brands will vary in how much water you may need to add for this dough to come together, so start with the amount listed above and then add 1 tablespoon at a time. It takes a solid 4 to 5 minutes to knead the dough, and somewhere in between this kneading is where you want to add additional water if needed. The dough should be supple but firm (soft pizza dough is not what we're looking for here) and should leave an indentation when pressed.

While you can now get frozen paratha and rotli in endless varieties at South Asian markets, I've always felt that knowing how to make from scratch this dish, a staple across many cultures in South Asia, is a key skill to have as a Gujarati—at least that's what my mom tells me. The truth is, paratha and rotli can take a little bit of patience to master, but this recipe calls for simple ingredients, and if you make them all at once in a batch for the week, it feels a lot less daunting and quite rewarding. I like these triangle-shaped paratha because there's less pressure to make them perfectly round, as with rotli, but they still taste great, and that's what truly matters. They're perfect to serve with any shaak, or vegetable dish, and you can even roll them up with a bit of ghee and gaur (jaggery) for a quick toddler treat. My favorite way to enjoy them is the next day, dipping each bite into Lasanyu Marchu (page 263) mixed with oil and flaky sea salt. SO GOOD. PS Don't get scared off by the directions below. The dough is very forgiving and makes this recipe easier than it sounds, promise! You can also cut this recipe in half for a smaller batch or keep the dough in the fridge for a few days; just bring it to room temperature before using. These can be made ahead of time and kept in an airtight container for 2 to 3 days in a cool, dark place. You can also keep these refrigerated and heat them up for a few seconds in the microwave before eating.

In a wide shallow bowl, combine the flour and salt, and using your hands, gently crush the ajwain seeds before adding them to the flour. Pour 2 tablespoons of the oil over the flour, and use your hands to mix the oil into the flour, breaking up any clumps. The dough should have a uniform sandy texture.

Add 1½ cups (360 ml) water to the flour mixture in small amounts and use your hands to knead the flour into a dough after each addition of water. Use your knuckles to press the dough, and continue to knead and fold and stretch the dough until uniform and smooth, without cracks, 4 to 5 minutes. If you still have dry bits of flour remaining in the bowl, add an additional tablespoon of water, swiping the ball of dough around the bowl to pick up any dried bits.

Move the dough onto a flat surface (sprinkle with some flour, if needed, to keep the dough from sticking). Press down on the dough to create a disc that is 1 inch (2.5 cm) thick all around and 6 inches (15 cm) in diameter. Using a bread scraper or large knife, cut the dough into quarters. Use your hands to roll each of the quarters into a 6-inch (15 cm) log, and then cut each log into 4 even pieces. Use your hands to shape each piece of dough into a round ball and set them aside on a large plate. You may need to lightly wet your hands to shape the dough into balls if the dough is resistant and too dry. Cover with a clean kitchen towel so the balls do not become dry.

To begin making the paratha, set up your workspace. You will need a small bowl of ghee and a shallow plate with the flour for dusting, a rolling pin, and a surface to roll the dough out.

Flatten one ball of dough between your palms, gently press each side of the dough into your plate of dusting flour and shake off any excess, then place the dough on your work surface.

Using your rolling pin, roll the dough out until it is a disc about 6 inches (15 cm) in diameter and even in thickness.

Using the tips of your fingers or a pastry brush, spread a thin layer of ghee over the dough, add a light sprinkle of atta over the ghee (this will help form flaky layers in the dough), then fold the dough into a half-moon shape. Add another thin layer of ghee over the half moon and a sprinkle of flour, and then fold it again into a triangular shape.

Press down on the dough, sprinkling some flour on your work surface if the dough begins to stick. Roll out the dough to about three times its size, or as thin as possible, trying to keep the triangular shape and using equal pressure to make sure the paratha is even in thickness. Repeat with the rest of the dough balls, rolling 2 to 3 at a time and laying them on a lightly floured surface while cooking them at the same time.

Heat a lightly oiled griddle or large pan over medium-high heat. Once the pan is hot, add the paratha. Drizzle ¼ teaspoon canola oil on top of the paratha. Once the underside of the paratha starts to get brown and ashy in spots, about 30 seconds, flip it. Cook for 10 seconds or so and drizzle another ¼ teaspoon of oil on the paratha and then flip it again, using a spatula to gently press down on the edges and rotating it as it cooks so it browns evenly. Flip again after a few seconds, and if there are any parts of the paratha that still look raw, press down with the spatula in those spots to help them cook. Remove from the pan once both sides are evenly browned. Repeat with the remaining paratha and serve warm or at room temperature.

See step-by-step photos on the following spread

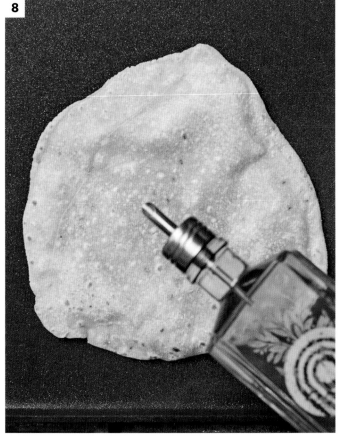

KALA CHANA NU SHAAK

Serves 4

1½ cups (280 g) dry kala chana (black chickpeas)

1¾ teaspoons salt

3 tablespoons canola or vegetable oil

1½ teaspoons cumin seeds

8 cloves garlic, roughly chopped

½ large onion, diced

¼ cup (35 g) besan (chickpea flour)

1 tablespoon red chili powder

1¼ teaspoons ground coriander

1¼ teaspoons ground cumin

1 teaspoon ground turmeric

2 teaspoons sugar

Juice of ½ lime

⅛ teaspoon garam masala

2 tablespoons finely chopped fresh cilantro

When I was growing up, my mom had a hard time getting me to eat my veggies. The only way I would eat them is if they were swimming in a puddle of gravy. One of the dishes I'd eat on repeat as a child is this kala chana nu shaak—black chickpeas in a delicious creamy curry sauce. Black chickpeas can be found at your local South Asian market or online and are smaller and denser than regular chickpeas. They also are firmer in texture, so they require soaking overnight and then pressure cooking to get them to soften. The gravy in this shaak is made with a roux of besan (chickpea flour) to create a thick, creamy consistency that is nutty, sweet, and slightly sour. This is delicious with Classic Paratha (page 174, or buy frozen paratha If you don't want to make the real ones—no shame in the game) or with a bowl of rice with some Classic Raita (page 259) on the side. It's great for meal prep for the week and freezes incredibly well, too!

Place the kala chana in a large bowl and cover with 2 inches (5 cm) water. Cover with foil and let soak overnight on the counter.

The next day, drain the soaked chana and add to an Instant Pot with 4 cups (960 ml) water and ½ teaspoon of the salt. Cook on high pressure for 30 minutes, then wait for a natural release before draining the chana. Set aside.

In a dutch oven or large pot, heat the oil over medium-high heat. Add the cumin seeds, and once they sizzle after a few seconds, add the garlic and cook until golden, about 1 minute. Lower the heat to medium, add the onion, and the remaining 1¼ teaspoons salt, and cook, stirring occasionally, for about 7 minutes, until they begin to brown. Add the besan and cook for about 4 minutes, until the flour no longer looks raw. Add the chili powder, coriander, cumin, and turmeric and continue to stir for about 1 minute.

Increase the heat to medium-high and add the chana. Add 2 cups (480 ml) water, stir, and slowly bring to a boil. Lower the temperature and simmer for about 5 minutes, or until the sauce thickens.

Add the sugar and lime juice and bring to a simmer, then reduce the heat to low and cook, covered, for about 5 minutes. Add the garam masala and cilantro and stir. Remove from the heat and serve.

MOM'S DAL FRY & JEERA RICE

Serves 4

1 cup (190 g) toor dal

½ teaspoon ground turmeric

2 teaspoons salt

3 tablespoons ghee

2 teaspoons cumin seeds

2 serrano chiles, finely chopped

½ teaspoon hing (asafetida)

6 large cloves garlic, chopped

8 to 10 curry leaves

1 medium yellow onion, diced

2 teaspoons red chili powder

1 teaspoon ground cumin

1 teaspoon ground coriander

3 tablespoons chopped fresh cilantro

1 recipe Jeera Rice (recipe follows)

NOTE

As the dal sits, it will start to thicken. You can add more water as needed when you reheat it (just be sure to adjust the salt level if you add a lot of water).

If you come to my house on a Monday, it's 100 percent likely that we're having dal fry and jeera rice for dinner. It's my cure-all meal after a weekend of indulging, or when we're returning home after a long vacation and our tummies need some gentle comfort food. While dal can be made with a variety of lentils, my mom's recipe uses toor dal, which I find to be simple and totally satisfying. I often refer to this dish as Indian soul food and a Patel family favorite, as my family has been eating it for generations. It is truly an heirloom recipe. I pour this over jeera rice, top it off with Chaat Onions (page 260), and have some papad (see headnote, page 153) on the side.

Rinse the toor dal with water a couple of times and then drain. Place the dal, 2 cups (480 ml) water, the turmeric, and 1 teaspoon of the salt into an Instant Pot. Set the mode to high pressure cook for 15 minutes and then quick release.

Heat a large pot over medium-high and add the ghee. Once it starts to melt, add the cumin seeds and serranos. Let them sizzle for a few seconds, then add the hing, garlic, and curry leaves. Stir continuously and let the garlic get slightly golden, 3 or 4 minutes.

Add the onion and the remaining 1 teaspoon salt and cook until the onions become translucent, about 5 minutes, then add the chili powder, cumin, and coriander. Stir, then add the cooked dal and 2½ cups (600 ml) water. Bring to a boil, reduce the heat, and simmer for 5 to 6 minutes.

Add the cilantro and serve the dal alongside the rice.

JEERA RICE

1   cup (180 g) long-grain basmati rice

1   tablespoon ghee

1½ teaspoons cumin seeds

2   whole cloves

2   bay leaves

½   teaspoon salt

Rinse the rice a few times, and then cover with water and let soak for 30 minutes. Drain the water and set aside.

In a medium pot, heat the ghee over medium-high heat. Add the cumin seeds and, once they begin to sizzle, add the cloves and bay leaves and give the spices a quick stir. Add the rice and toast, stirring constantly, for about 2 minutes. Add 2 cups (480 ml) water and the salt and bring to a rolling boil. Cover and reduce the heat to low. Cook for about 12 minutes, or until the rice is fluffy and all of the water has been absorbed. Fluff with a fork right before serving.

CHAAT

Serves 4, generously

- 2 large peeled potatoes, cooked whole and, once cooled, diced small
- 1 teaspoon ground cumin
- ½ teaspoon red chili powder
- ½ teaspoon black salt (or increase the chaat masala and plain salt)
- ¾ teaspoon salt
- 2 (14-ounce/400 g) boxes store-bought chaat papdi
- 1 cup (240 ml) Yogurt Chutney (page 194), or more to taste
- 1 teaspoon chaat masala
- ½ cup (120 ml) Cilantro Chutney (page 193), or more to taste
- ½ cup (120 ml) Tamarind Date Chutney (page 195), or more to taste
- ¼ cup (120 ml) Spicy Garlic Chutney (page 195), or more to taste
- 1 large red onion, diced
- 1⅓ cups (120 g) store-bought thin sev
- ½ cup (20 g) finely chopped fresh cilantro
- 1 cup (140 g) pomegranate seeds

PRO TIP

To make these chutneys a bit more spreadable, add 1 to 2 tablespoons of water to them so they're easier to drizzle and spread!

Samosa chaat, papdi chaat, katori chaat, spinach chaat, kale chaat . . . you get where I'm going with this? There are a ton of different ways you can make chaat, and I could not put a cookbook out into the world without giving you a recipe for this classic snack! You'll see that the base (made with potatoes here) is quite simple, and the magic is truly in the chutneys that are layered in this dish, so that every bite is sweet, spicy, sour, and oh so savory! My advice is to prepare the chutneys a few days ahead to make this less fussy (you could also prepare them weeks to months in advance, freeze them, and defrost twenty-four hours prior to serving). Also, the amounts listed for the chutneys are approximate, and more or less to taste. Since the chutneys can be a little time-consuming, my family has always used store-bought papdi, readily available at most South Asian markets. If you cannot find them near you or online, cut store-bought flour tortillas into little diamond shapes with a pizza cutter and deep-fry or bake them until crispy, as a quick alternative. And if you really wanna take the easy easy easy way out, cook up some frozen samosa, pile on all the chutneys, and call it a day, friend. Like I said, the magic is in the chutneys, and I've got you covered on that!

Combine the diced potatoes with the cumin, chili powder, black salt, and salt, until mixed together well.

To assemble the four chaats, set out four dinner plates. Gently break up about 10 papdi and place on each individual plate. Then on top of each papdi, layer ½ cup (65 g) of the potato mixture, ¼ cup (60 ml) yogurt chutney, ¼ teaspoon chaat masala, 2 tablespoons cilantro chutney, 2 tablespoons tamarind date chutney, 1 tablespoon garlic chutney, 2 tablespoons onion, ⅓ cup (30 g) sev, 2 tablespoons cilantro, and ¼ cup (35 g) pomegranate seeds, spreading everything out evenly. Repeat with the remaining chaat and toppings. Serve immediately.

CHAAT &
PAKORA *PARTY*

I will always choose snacks over a meal, apps over a main course, and because my family is the same way, we often make an entire dinner out of chaat and bhajiya, two extremely popular snack foods across many parts of India, and for good reason. Crispy, savory, sweet, spicy, sour, they hit ALL the cravings. Kasturi onion bhajiya are a family recipe we make often with chaat—eating them piping hot batch after batch. Truthfully, after a big plate of chaat, and a few bhajiya, it's pretty hard to eat anything else! It's a must-have Friday night treat for all of us, and when my mom and masi visit, this is always one of their top requests, because it's something they are constantly making for others and never for themselves! The chutneys for chaat may seem time consuming, but I always make these a day or two before or a couple weeks ahead and freeze them, which makes prep on the day of so much easier.

Kasturi Onion Bhajiya 186

Pineapple Mojitos 190

FOR THE CHAAT

Cilantro Chutney 193

Yogurt Chutney 194

Spicy Garlic Chutney 195

Tamarind Date Chutney 195

Pomegranate seeds, diced onions,
and fresh cilantro

Sev, chaat papdi, and/or puri
(see pantry, page 20)

KASTURI ONION BHAJIYA

Makes 18 to 20 fritters; serves 4

Bhajiya are hands down the quintessential Gujarati snack. Weddings, rainy days, picnic—we find any excuse to fry up some fritters! While there are a ton of versions, I love these onion bhajiya for how crunchy and simple they are. Efficiency is key when you're deep-frying, so I recommend setting up the mise en place (all of the things that you will need) before you start. I like to fry a small batch first to taste for salt and spice, and then adjust the batter as needed before frying more. Sweet Vidalia onions are my favorite for these because they help balance all of the other peppery ingredients! Also, while the eight Thai green chiles in this recipe may sound like a lot, the chiles lose a bit of their heat when they hit the hot oil, so add more or less based on your preference. I love serving these with Tarragon Aioli (page 256) or with Cilantro Jalapeño Sauce (page 252) mixed with a bit of yogurt.

2	large sweet onions, sliced into 2 by ¼–inch (5 cm by 6 mm) strips
8	Thai green chiles, finely chopped
2	tablespoons whole coriander, lightly crushed in a mortar and pestle or smashed with a rolling pin
2	teaspoons cumin seeds
2	teaspoons coarsely ground black pepper
¼	cup (40 g) rice flour
2	cups (180 g) besan (chickpea flour)
2	teaspoons red chili powder
¼	teaspoon hing (asafetida)
½	heaping cup (about 45 g) finely chopped fresh cilantro
2½	teaspoons salt
¼	teaspoon ground turmeric
2	teaspoons garlic powder
	Canola oil, for frying
	Black salt, for sprinkling

In a large bowl, combine all of the ingredients except for the black salt and canola oil. Use your hands to toss and massage this mixture for about 2 minutes. As you massage everything, the salt will help release moisture from the onions. Next, add 3 tablespoons water, 1 tablespoon at a time, mixing the water in with your hands after each addition. Add the water until there is no longer any dry flour or ingredients at the bottom of the bowl and the batter is thick and sticky. You may need to add more water to achieve this—it's dependent on the brand of flour you use, as well as the liquid released by the onions.

Add enough canola oil to a medium-size pot to come 3 inches (7.5 cm) up the side and heat over medium-high to 350°F (175°C), testing with a candy thermometer or by dropping a bit of the onion mixture into the hot oil. If it rises fairly quickly, the oil is ready.

Use your fingertips to gather some of the onion mixture into a small clump, then drop it carefully into the hot oil. If you're nervous about getting splattered with the oil, you can use a spoon to gather a small cluster of onion mixture, then use a second spoon to break it loose and drop it into the oil.

You will want to add a few bhajiya at a time, as many as fit with room for you to still be able to gently move them around, so they don't stick or crowd the pan. Use a spider or slotted metal spatula to gently turn the bhajiya, so they cook evenly on both sides, about 2 minutes per side. I like to test one carefully to make sure it's not raw inside.

Once the fritters are golden brown, remove them from the oil and place on a large paper towel–lined platter. Reduce the heat as needed if bhajiya are browning too fast, which will result in the outside being browned but the onions remaining too raw.

As you remove each batch from the oil, sprinkle lightly (or generously) with black salt for extra kick—don't skip this step!

PRO TIPS

Here are a few tips for optimal frying.

1. Make sure the oil is HOT. You don't want your oil to be smoking, but as it heats, drop little bits of the batter into the oil, and when they instantly rise to the top, you know the oil is hot enough for frying. If your fritters are turning too golden too fast, reduce the heat and wait for the oil to cool down a bit. Otherwise, you will end up with a very golden exterior but uncooked and raw onions on the inside.

2. Use the proper tools! A stainless-steel spider spatula or one in the shape of a basket is key for removing the fritters from the hot oil and transferring them safely onto a plate (plus the slots help drain excess oil).

3. Set up your workspace in advance of frying—this helps keep things tidy and accident-free. You'll need a spider spatula, a damp towel to wipe your hands on after you've dropped the batter in the oil and need a clean hand to hold the spatula, a large plate lined with paper towels, and some black salt placed in a shaker bottle or in a bowl so you can sprinkle it over the hot bhajiya.

PINEAPPLE MOJITOS

Makes 8 drinks

Bright and refreshing, these puckery pineapple cocktails are a hit any time of year, but we especially love them during the summer. They are light, juicy, and the one cocktail I can convince my mom to sip on, because with all the fresh mint and lime, you can barely taste the rum!

- 6 ounces (180 ml) fresh lime juice
- ¼ cup (50 g) sugar
- 40 fresh mint leaves, plus sprigs for garnish
- 1 quart (about 1 L) white rum
- 1 quart (about 1 L) fresh pineapple juice
- 8 ounces (240 ml) club soda

In a large jar, add the lime juice, sugar, and mint leaves. Using a muddler or wooden kitchen spoon, muddle or crush the mint to bruise the leaves. Stir until the sugar has dissolved.

Pour the lime juice and mint mixture and the rum and pineapple juice into a large pitcher.

Keep the mojito mixture in the fridge until ready to serve. Pour into Tom Collins glasses filled with ice, about three-fourths of the way full. Briskly stir the drinks, top each with a splash of soda water, and serve with the mint garnish.

CILANTRO CHUTNEY

Makes 1¼ cups (300 ml)

Growing up, when I was cooking and something didn't taste quite right, I was known for adding a spoonful of my mom's chutney to improve most any dish. Hers was the best, hands down. Not too watery, not too thick, not too tart. It was spicy, garlicky, and so potent that a little bit went a long way. I mix this with mayo for a delicious sandwich spread, or add a spoonful to my toddler's chicken noodle soup for an instant adult-friendly upgrade. You'll find it in my Samosa Grilled Cheese (page 109), and I even add a spoonful to my Hot & Cheesy Corn Dip (page 229). This recipe makes a big batch, and rather than let it sit in the fridge for a few days, I usually freeze the majority of it in ice cube trays. Once the cubes have set, pop them out and put them into a resealable plastic bag to keep in the freezer. Grab a cube and defrost it whenever you need some.

2   bunches roughly chopped fresh cilantro leaves with 2 inches (5 cm) of the stems (about 4 cups/160 g)

6   cloves garlic, peeled

1   (½-inch/12 mm) piece fresh ginger

3   or 4 serrano chiles

1   teaspoon ground cumin

    Juice from 1 lime

3   tablespoons raw peanuts

¾   teaspoon salt, plus more as needed

In a small food processor or blender, combine the cilantro, garlic, ginger, serranos, cumin, lime juice, peanuts, and salt and blend until smooth.

Add 1 to 2 tablespoons of water at a time, scraping down the sides of the blender with a spatula, until the chutney moves easily in the blender. Taste for spice, adding more chiles and salt as needed. Refrigerate for up to a week or freeze.

YOGURT CHUTNEY

Makes 1½ cups (360 ml)

This yogurt chutney is super simple and what my family uses in recipes such as Chaat (page 183). It's just plain yogurt spruced up with a few simple spices!

1½ cups (360 ml) whole-milk plain yogurt

½ teaspoon salt

½ teaspoon sugar

½ teaspoon ground cumin

⅛ teaspoon red chili powder

In a medium bowl, whisk together the yogurt, salt, sugar, cumin, and chili powder. Refrigerate for up to a week.

SPICY GARLIC CHUTNEY

Makes 3 cups (720 ml)

For an extra kick of garlic and chiles, my family and I use this in and on everything from falafel to chaat, from tacos and enchiladas to Chicken Pita Wraps with Tomato Onion Salad & Tzatziki (page 209). This recipe will vary in spice level based on how spicy your dried red chiles are. I like to think of this as a "little goes a long way" sort of condiment, so you don't want to drench your food in it, but a few little drizzles to add heat is perfect. This freezes very well, or refrigerate it for up to a week.

16 dried red chiles, soaked in hot water in a covered pot for at least 3 hours

3 red bell peppers

1½ teaspoons cumin seeds

6 cloves garlic, peeled

¾ teaspoon salt, plus more if needed

Drain the red chiles, remove and discard the stems, and blot off any excess water with a paper towel or kitchen towel.

In a blender, combine the rehydrated chiles, bell peppers, cumin seeds, garlic, and salt and blend on high speed until completely smooth. (You may have to add 1 to 2 tablespoons of water to get the blender going, depending on how juicy your peppers are.) Taste for salt and adjust if needed, transfer to a sealed glass container, and refrigerate for up to a week.

TAMARIND DATE CHUTNEY

Makes 4 cups (about 1 L)

There are certain dishes that have easy shortcuts, but I hear my mom's voice in the back of my head telling me I should at least know how to make the real, more laborious version, so here we are. This Tamarind Date Chutney is one of those core recipes I really wanted to get under my belt. It felt so intimidating at first, but I was surprised at how quickly it comes together. Jaggery has a rich molasses flavor and is traditionally used in place of sugar in many Indian recipes. You can enjoy this sweet chutney in Samosa Grilled Cheese (page 109) and Chaat (page 183), and because it makes a big ole batch, feel free to halve this recipe or freeze the extra!

1 (3-ounce/85 g) block seedless tamarind (about ⅓ cup)

6 ounces (170 g) pitted dates (about 25 dates)

4 cups (about 1 L) hot water

1¼ cups (140 g) grated jaggery or white or packed brown sugar

1½ tablespoons ground cumin

1 tablespoon red chili powder

1 teaspoon black salt (see page 16)

Place the tamarind and dates in bowl with the hot water, cover, and let soak for 30 minutes. Transfer the tamarind and dates with their soaking water to a high-speed blender. Blend on high for about 1 minute, until the mixture is completely smooth. You may have to do this in batches.

Set a fine-mesh strainer over a medium saucepan and pour the tamarind and date mixture through the strainer in batches, using a spatula to gently push the mixture through the strainer. Discard any pulp left in the strainer.

Heat the saucepan over medium heat, add the jaggery, and bring to a boil, stirring occasionally to melt the jaggery. Reduce the heat to low and let the mixture simmer, stirring frequently, for about 5 minutes. It may bubble and will be very hot, so be careful.

Add the cumin, chili powder, and black salt and cook for an additional 2 to 3 minutes. Remove the pan from the heat and let cool. The chutney will continue to thicken as it sits. Once cool, transfer to a sealed container and keep refrigerated for up to a week, or freeze in small batches.

Chandani is technically my cousin, but we fight like sisters. She is my sous chef for life!

NON-VEG

While I eat a mostly vegetarian diet, I wanted to include a chapter with some of my favorite chicken, turkey, fish, shellfish, lamb, and pork dishes as well. Meat is eaten widely across many regions in India. While I know a lot of Gujarati people don't eat much meat, my family and the community I grew up in did. I usually cook meat two to three times a week, often pairing it with a vegetable side dish or a soup to round out the meal. If I'm hosting a dinner or party, the meal is likely 70 percent vegetarian with a few non-veg options thrown in for variety and to satisfy everyone's preferences.

What I love about many of the recipes in this chapter is that they turn into a base for different meals throughout the week. I often make double batches of proteins and toss them into a salad, a grain bowl, or a wrap or quesadilla. Indian spices are an especially good complement to roasted or grilled meats, delivering maximum flavor, like the smokiness from cumin and coriander that creates something special and surprising in every bite of my turkey burgers. A BLT becomes something off the hook when you turn regular bacon into sweet-and-spicy candied bacon.

These dishes also work well as part of an entertaining spread. Coconut Shrimp Po' Boys with Panang Curry Remoulade (page 206), Crispy Barbecue Chicken Kheema Tacos (page 210), and Korean-Inspired Baked Wings (page 214) are all awesome to serve while watching a game on a Sunday afternoon. If I were hosting an intimate dinner party, One-Pan Salmon & Spinach (page 202) would definitely be on the menu. And if you want to stick to non-meat, many of the recipes in this chapter can be easily adjusted to be fully plant-based by swapping in meaty roasted vegetables like portobello mushrooms, eggplant, or even lentils and tofu to replace ground meat.

Panko-Crusted HALIBUT

with JAMMY HARISSA TOMATOES

Serves 4

¾ cup (60 g) panko breadcrumbs

2 tablespoons fresh parsley, finely chopped

3 cloves garlic, grated

1 lemon

½ cup (50 g) grated Pecorino Romano cheese

¼ cup (60 ml) plus 3 tablespoons extra-virgin olive oil

Salt and freshly ground black pepper

1½ pounds (680 g) cherry tomatoes, halved

3 tablespoons harissa sauce (I like Mina brand)

¼ cup (10 g) chopped fresh basil

4 (6-ounce/170 g) skinless halibut fillets

PRO TIP

Test for doneness by making a small incision in the center of the fillets; the flesh should be opaque. Be sure to check each fillet, as they do not all cook at the same rate; remove those that are done and keep them warm as one or two may need an additional minute to finish cooking.

When I first made this dish, my cousin Chandani took a bite, looked at me, and said, "This feels like something that would be served at a fancy dinner party. But, like, it actually tastes good!" Whenever I eat fish, it's usually great for the first few bites but it's never so indulgent or satisfying that I want to polish off the entire portion. But when it comes to this halibut, I find myself with an empty bowl, debating if I should go for seconds! The cherry tomatoes get a head start in the oven, where they magically transform into jammy, brothy goodness that you can serve with rice or pasta to round out the meal. You can also swap out the halibut for snapper, tuna, flounder, or swordfish.

Preheat the oven to 400°F (205°C).

In a small bowl, mix the breadcrumbs, parsley, garlic, zest of the lemon, Pecorino Romano, 3 tablespoons of the oil, ½ teaspoon salt, and black pepper to taste. Set aside.

In a 9 by 13–inch (23 by 33 cm) baking dish, combine remaining ¼ cup (60 ml) oil, the tomatoes, harissa, basil, and ¾ teaspoon salt. Toss to combine. Cover tightly with foil and roast for 20 minutes. Remove from the oven and lower the temperature to 375°F (190°C).

Squeeze the juice of the lemon onto both sides of the fillets, and then sprinkle the fillets with salt and pepper. Evenly distribute the breadcrumb mixture on the tops of the fillets, pressing down gently so the breadcrumbs adhere. Carefully transfer each fillet to the baking dish, on top of the tomato mixture. Bake the fish, uncovered, until the flesh is opaque when pierced with a knife, 15 to 20 minutes.

Carefully transfer the fish to individual serving bowls and spoon some of the tomato mixture around each fillet. Serve immediately.

One-Pan
SALMON &
SPINACH

Serves 4

- 1½ teaspoons ground paprika
- 2 teaspoons garlic powder
- 2 teaspoons onion powder
- 1 teaspoon dried thyme
- ¼ teaspoon freshly ground black pepper
- ½ teaspoon salt
- 4 (6-ounce/170 g) skinless salmon fillets
- 2 tablespoons canola or vegetable oil
- 2 cups loosely packed (40 g) baby spinach leaves
- 2 tablespoons finely chopped fresh parsley, for garnish

For the sauce

- 2 tablespoons unsalted butter
- 6 cloves garlic, grated
- 1 cup (240 ml) vegetable or chicken broth
- 1 cup (240 ml) heavy cream
- ½ teaspoon ground paprika
- ½ teaspoon garlic powder
- 1 teaspoon Dijon mustard
- 1 teaspoon Worcestershire sauce
- ½ teaspoon salt
- 2 teaspoons fresh lemon juice

Chances are, if you come to my house for a dinner party, I'll be serving this dish as part of a larger meal. It's rich and decadent, and one of the few recipes in this book that doesn't call for Indian flavors or spices. The combination of velvety salmon, mustard-garlic cream sauce, and silky spinach doesn't need any heat to deliver great taste. It is perfect paired with Buttery Bowties & Matar (page 125).

In a small bowl, mix together the paprika, garlic powder, onion powder, thyme, pepper, and salt. Make sure the salmon fillets are completely dry, and then pat the seasoning blend onto both sides of each fillet.

Heat the oil in a large cast-iron skillet over medium-high heat. Add the salmon and cook for about 3 minutes, or until it has developed a nice sear on the bottom. Carefully flip each fillet and cook for another 3 minutes, until the flesh is opaque when pierced with a knife. Transfer the salmon to a plate and reduce the heat to medium-low.

MAKE THE SAUCE: Add the butter and garlic to the skillet, and whisk for about 30 seconds, taking care not to burn the garlic. Slowly whisk in the broth, taking care to scrape up any browned bits on the bottom of the pan. Bring to a simmer, then reduce the heat to medium-low. Whisk in the heavy cream, paprika, garlic powder, mustard, Worcestershire, salt, and lemon juice and simmer until the sauce begins to thicken slightly, 2 to 3 minutes.

Add the spinach to the skillet and stir until wilted.

Return the salmon to the skillet. Cover and cook for an additional 2 to 3 minutes, testing after 3 minutes by gently piercing the flesh with a knife. It should be opaque. Transfer the salmon and spinach to a serving platter and spoon the sauce over the top. Garnish with parsley and serve.

MASALA SHRIMP SCAMPI

Serves 4

1 pound (455 g) shrimp, peeled and deveined with tails intact

2 teaspoons ground cumin

2 teaspoons red chili powder

1 teaspoon salt, plus more if needed

2 tablespoons extra-virgin olive oil

½ red bell pepper, sliced

½ green bell pepper, sliced

1 tablespoon tomato paste

6 cloves garlic, grated

1 teaspoon ground coriander

1 teaspoon garam masala

1 teaspoon tandoori masala

1 teaspoon Old Bay seasoning

½ teaspoon ground turmeric

3 tablespoons unsalted butter

½ cup (120 ml) white wine

½ cup (120 ml) vegetable broth or water

2 tablespoons lemon juice

3 tablespoons finely chopped fresh parsley

I love shrimp that is juicy, saucy, and super garlicky. My take on traditional scampi amps up the heat and flavor to the max, so this dish tends to disappear from the table really, really fast. It's especially perfect paired with Hangover Spaghetti (page 120), and works well as an appetizer, served with crusty bread to soak up the delicious sauce.

In a large bowl, toss the shrimp with the cumin, chili powder, and salt and set aside.

Heat a large pot or wok over medium-high and add the oil. Once the oil is hot, add the red and green peppers and cook for 2 to 3 minutes. Stir in the tomato paste and garlic and cook for 3 to 4 minutes, until the garlic is fragrant. Add the coriander, garam masala, tandoori masala, Old Bay seasoning, and turmeric and cook for 2 to 3 minutes.

Add the butter to the pan. When melted, add the shrimp and gently stir to combine. Cook for 2 to 3 minutes. Add the wine and cook for 1 minute to reduce slightly. Add the broth, turn the heat down to low, cover the pot, and cook for another 2 minutes, until the shrimp are pink in color and cooked through.

Turn off the heat and stir in the lemon juice and parsley. Taste for salt and adjust as needed. Serve immediately.

COCONUT SHRIMP PO' BOYS

with PANANG CURRY REMOULADE

Serves 4

For the remoulade

- 1½ cups (360 ml) mayonnaise
- 3 tablespoons store-bought panang curry paste
- 2 cloves garlic, grated
- 2 serrano chiles, finely chopped
- 2 tablespoons finely chopped fresh cilantro (leaves and tender stems)
- 1 tablespoon chopped cornichons, gherkins, or half-sour pickles
- 1 tablespoon chopped capers
- Zest and juice of ½ lime

For the sandwiches

- 1 pound (455 g) large shrimp (26 to 30 count), peeled and deveined
- Salt
- ½ teaspoon cayenne pepper
- ½ teaspoon ground cumin
- ½ teaspoon ground coriander
- 1 cup (130 g) cornstarch
- Freshly ground black pepper
- 4 egg whites
- 1½ cups (120 g) panko breadcrumbs
- 1 cup (85 g) shredded unsweetened coconut
- ¼ cup (60 ml) unrefined/virgin coconut oil
- ¼ cup (60 ml) canola oil
- 4 (6-inch/15 cm) hero rolls, halved lengthwise
- 2 cups loosely packed (40 g) baby arugula
- ½ lime for squeezing, plus lime wedges for serving
- ¼ cup (10 g) finely chopped fresh cilantro

These sandwiches make for a satisfying lunch or game-day meal. The flavor of the remoulade builds as it sits, so plan on making it ahead, even the night before. Like me, you will no doubt find it addictive, and want to try it on everything from grilled fish and chicken to tacos. I used a mixture of coconut and canola oil here for maximum coconut flavor, but you can just use canola oil if that's what you have on hand. And feel free to lose the rolls and serve just the coconut shrimp, as an app or to top off a salad, but don't skip the remoulade—it's the star! Serve these po' boys with Too Good to Be True Corn Soup (page 68) for a perfect summer combo.

MAKE THE REMOULADE: In a small bowl, combine the mayonnaise, curry paste, garlic, serranos, cilantro, cornichons, capers, and lime zest and juice and mix well. Set aside.

MAKE THE SANDWICHES: Toss the shrimp with 1 teaspoon salt, the cayenne, cumin, and coriander.

Set out three shallow bowls: Fill the first with the cornstarch, seasoned with salt and pepper; the second with the egg whites, whipped lightly with a whisk; and the third with the breadcrumbs and coconut, stirred to combine.

Lightly dredge a few shrimp in the cornstarch, then pat off the excess; dip in the egg white, then lightly shake off the excess; dip in the coconut-panko mixture, and gently press the mixture on both sides to adhere. Set aside on a plate and repeat until all the shrimp are coated.

Mix together the coconut oil and canola oil in a small bowl. Add ¼ cup (60 ml) of the combined oil to a large skillet or cooking pan over medium-high heat. To test the heat of the oil, drop a pinch of coconut in the oil. When it sizzles, add a batch of the shrimp, being careful not to crowd the pan, and cook, 1 to 2 minutes per side, until the shrimp are golden and firm. Transfer the shrimp to a paper towel–lined tray. Repeat with the remaining shrimp, adding more of the oil to the pan as needed.

To assemble the sandwiches, spread remoulade on both sides of each roll. Top the bottom halves with the baby arugula and a squeeze of lime. Top with the shrimp, more lime juice if desired, and chopped cilantro, and close the sandwiches. Serve with lime wedges.

CHICKEN PITA WRAPS

with TOMATO ONION SALAD & TZATZIKI

Serves 4

For the marinade

- 4 serrano chiles, stemmed
- 8 cloves garlic, peeled
- 1 (1-inch/2.5 cm) piece fresh ginger
- ½ cup (120 ml) whole-milk plain yogurt
- 1 tablespoon salt
- 2 teaspoons onion powder
- 1 teaspoon chaat masala
- ½ teaspoon freshly ground black pepper
- 1 teaspoon ground turmeric
- 2 teaspoons red chili powder
- 2 teaspoons ground coriander
- 2 teaspoons ground cumin
- ¼ teaspoon ground cinnamon
- 1 tablespoon garam masala
- 1 tablespoon canola or vegetable oil
- 2 tablespoons cream cheese, softened

For the chicken wraps

- 2 pounds (910 g) boneless, skinless chicken thighs (8 thighs)
- Olive oil
- 6 plum tomatoes, cored and diced
- ½ red onion, thinly sliced
- 1 teaspoon Aleppo pepper
- 1 teaspoon za'atar
- 1 teaspoon salt
- 2 tablespoons finely chopped fresh cilantro, mint, or parsley
- 2 teaspoons red wine vinegar
- 1 teaspoon fresh lime juice
- 4 pitas
- Tzatziki (page 257)

This Greek-inspired recipe is ideal for summertime grilling, but you can enjoy it year-round by using a grill pan or cast-iron skillet on your stovetop. I prefer chicken thighs for this recipe, as they tend to have more flavor, don't dry out, and for my novice meat makers, they're hard to overcook! I always make a second batch of this chicken to use throughout the week in salads, grain bowls, with rice, you name it. And if you like a little more heat, try adding a teaspoon of Lasanyu Marchu (page 263) to the tzatziki.

MAKE THE MARINADE: Place all of the marinade ingredients in a food processor and process until smooth.

MAKE THE CHICKEN WRAPS: Place the chicken thighs in a large, wide bowl or shallow baking dish and pour the marinade over the top, making sure each piece is generously coated. Cover and refrigerate the chicken for a few hours or overnight.

When ready to cook the chicken, heat 2 tablespoons olive oil in a large grill pan or cast-iron pan over medium-high heat. Add just 3 or 4 thighs to the pan (do not crowd the pan, as you don't want the chicken to steam) and cook for 5 to 6 minutes on each side, keeping an eye on the heat, until the chicken develops a nice char. Repeat with the remaining chicken, adding additional oil to the pan as needed. Allow the chicken to rest on a plate for 5 minutes. Cut into bite-size pieces.

Combine the tomatoes, onion, Aleppo pepper, za'atar, salt, cilantro, vinegar, and lime juice in a medium bowl and toss to mix.

To assemble the wraps, lightly warm the pitas in a skillet, about a minute on each side. Spread the pitas with tzatziki, top with the chicken, dividing it equally among the wraps, and garnish with the tomato and onion salad. Serve immediately. You can enjoy these open-face or gently folded. You can also stuff the chicken and salad into pita pockets, if you prefer.

PRO TIP

The chicken should marinate for a few hours or overnight and can then be made ahead of time. When ready to assemble the pitas, give the chicken a quick reheat on a hot, lightly oiled grill or cast-iron pan for a minute or two or until warm.

Crispy
BARBECUE CHICKEN
KHEEMA TACOS

with AVOCADO-ORANGE SALSA

Serves 4

For the salsa

- 2 oranges, peeled, seeded, and diced
- 2 large ripe avocados, pitted and diced
- 2 jalapeño chiles, seeded and finely chopped
- ½ cup (20 g) finely chopped fresh cilantro
- 2 tablespoons fresh lime juice
- ½ cup (65 g) thinly sliced red onion
- ½ teaspoon ground cumin
- ½ teaspoon salt
-    Freshly ground black pepper

For the tacos

- 3 tablespoons (60 ml) canola or vegetable oil, plus more for frying
- 1 bay leaf
- 1 teaspoon cumin seeds
- 2 serrano chiles (or 3 to 4 jalapeño chiles), finely diced
- 1 cup (110 g) diced onion
- 1 tablespoon minced garlic
- 2 teaspoons minced fresh ginger
- 1 pound (455 g) ground chicken
- 1 teaspoon red chili powder
- 2 teaspoons ground coriander
- 2 teaspoons ground cumin
- 2 teaspoons garam masala
- ½ cup (120 ml) prepared barbecue sauce
- 1 tablespoon fresh lime juice

While I'm typically not a fan of barbecue sauce, I have come to LOVE these tacos, which feature it as their secret ingredient. The burst of juicy citrus from the oranges and the rich mellowness of the avocado pair with the smokiness of the barbecue sauce to create an unexpected yet perfectly balanced bite—unreal! I like to keep this recipe up my sleeve for entertaining because people respond to the wow factor these tacos deliver. Top them with the kheema and salsa and you've got bite-size tostadas. This recipe scales up really well, so it's great for a crowd. You can also double the chicken and freeze half. It defrosts quickly; serve it over rice with a vegetable for a busy weeknight dinner. And if you want to turn this into a super cute open-face app, use a cookie cutter to cut 2-inch (5 cm) rounds out of the corn tortillas, cut a few slits in each one, and then deep-fry them.

MAKE THE SALSA: Add the oranges, avocados, jalapeños, cilantro, lime juice, onion, cumin, salt, and pepper to taste to a serving bowl and mix gently to combine. Refrigerate until ready to serve.

MAKE THE TACOS: Heat the oil in a large, wide skillet with tall sides over medium-high heat. Add the bay leaf and cumin seeds and let cook for about 20 seconds. Add the serranos and cook for a few seconds. Add the onion and cook for 3 to 5 minutes, stirring often, until the onion is translucent and golden around the edges. Add the garlic and ginger and stir for 1 minute, until the garlic is fragrant, but not browned. Reduce the heat if necessary to keep the garlic from browning.

Add the ground chicken to the pan, along with the chili powder, coriander, cumin, and garam masala. Stir the mixture and break up the chicken into small pieces. Once the chicken begins to brown, stir in the barbecue sauce and lime juice and continue to cook over medium-low heat for 5 to 6 minutes, until the chicken is cooked through and no longer pink. Stir in the cilantro and remove from the heat.

To assemble the tacos, wrap the corn tortillas in a damp paper towel and cook them in a microwave for 10 seconds; this will make them more pliable and prevent them from breaking.

Heat a large skillet over medium-high heat and add about ½ teaspoon oil. Place one or two tortillas in the skillet and top half of each one with a scoop of the chicken kheema and a handful of shredded cheese. Using a spatula, fold over the other half to create a half-moon shape. With the spatula, gently hold the tortilla in place to close. Check the underside and flip once the bottom side is browned. Cook for another minute or two and transfer the taco to a platter. Repeat with the remaining tortillas, chicken kheema, and cheese, adding more oil as needed. Place the tacos on a platter and serve with the salsa alongside.

¼   cup (10 g) finely chopped fresh cilantro

8   corn tortillas

8   ounces (225 g) pepper Jack or Monterey Jack cheese, coarsely shredded (about 1¾ cups)

Sweet & Spicy
TURKEY MEATBALLS
with NOODLES

Serves 4

For the sauce

⅓ cup (75 ml) hoisin sauce

1 tablespoon rice wine vinegar

2 tablespoons gochujang (Korean chili paste)

¼ cup (60 ml) sweet Thai chili sauce

2 tablespoons soy sauce

1 tablespoon sesame oil

2 teaspoons toasted sesame seeds

For the meatballs

1 pound (455 g) ground turkey

6 cloves garlic

1 (1-inch/2.5 cm) piece fresh ginger

1 serrano chile

¼ cup (10 g) roughly chopped fresh cilantro (leaves and tender stems)

1 bunch green onions, thinly sliced

¼ cup (20 g) panko breadcrumbs

¾ teaspoon salt

1 tablespoon soy sauce

4 tablespoons (60 ml) canola or vegetable oil, plus more as needed

For serving

8 ounces (225 g) cooked fresh ramen, or noodles of your choice

2 Persian cucumbers, cut into 1-inch (2.5 cm) matchsticks

Toasted sesame seeds

I have been known to eat noodles for breakfast, in desperate situations with my hands—but that's a story for another day and one that probably doesn't need to live in print! To appease Pinank and his ridiculously fast metabolism, I often make these turkey meatballs and noodles. They're sweet, spicy, and contain a lot of Asian influences such as the sesame oil, hoisin, and gochujang, all of which bring a depth of flavor that is way better than takeout. Fresh noodles from your local Asian market make a world of difference, so try to get the good stuff, and grab an extra packet so you can freeze it and defrost it for next time. If you're vegetarian, skip the meatballs and toss in some mushrooms and bok choy.

Preheat the oven to 425°F (220°C).

MAKE THE SAUCE: In a small bowl, mix together the hoisin, rice wine vinegar, gochujang, chili sauce, soy sauce, sesame oil, and sesame seeds.

MAKE THE MEATBALLS: Place the ground turkey in a large bowl. In a small food processor, combine the garlic, ginger, serrano, cilantro, and half of the green onions and blend until everything is finely chopped. Add all but 2 tablespoons of this mixture to the ground turkey, along with the breadcrumbs, salt, soy sauce, and remaining half of the green onions. Use your hands to lightly mix everything together.

Lightly oil your hands and form the turkey mixture into small meatballs, about 1 inch (2.5 cm) in diameter. You should have about 22 meatballs.

Heat 1 tablespoon of the oil in a large cast-iron skillet or dutch oven over medium-high heat. Add half the meatballs and sear on all sides, 4 to 6 minutes total. Transfer to a large baking sheet. Add 1 tablespoon of the oil to the skillet and repeat with the remaining meatballs.

Bake the meatballs for 6 to 8 minutes, until their juices run clear when pierced.

Meanwhile in a large skillet, heat the remaining 2 tablespoons oil over medium heat. Add the remaining 2 tablespoons of the garlic-ginger mixture, stirring often, until fragrant and slightly golden, 1 to 2 minutes.

Reduce the heat to low. Add the sauce and cooked noodles, and with tongs, mix to evenly coat the noodles with the sauce.

Gently mix the cooked meatballs with the noodles. Divide
among 4 pasta bowls. Garnish with the remaining green
onions, the cucumbers, and sesame seeds and serve.

Korean-Inspired BAKED WINGS

Serves 4

For the wings

- 2 pounds (910 g) chicken wings
- 2 tablespoons aluminum-free baking powder
- 1 teaspoon salt
- ½ teaspoon freshly ground black pepper

For the sauce

- ⅓ cup (95 g) gochujang (Korean chili paste)
- 1 tablespoon gochugaru (Korean chili powder)
- 3 tablespoons mayonnaise
- 2 tablespoons rice wine vinegar
- 3 tablespoons toasted sesame oil
- 3 tablespoons minced fresh ginger
- 3 tablespoons minced garlic
- 3 tablespoons packed brown sugar
- 2 tablespoons honey

For serving

- Toasted sesame seeds
- ¼ cup (15 g) chopped green onion
- Cilantro Jalapeño Sauce (page 252)

Whether you're watching a Sunday afternoon football game or looking for something fun to make for lunch for the kids, it's hard to resist these savory wings. The secret ingredient that makes them super crispy is baking powder. Tossing the wings in baking powder before they hit the oven helps deliver a whole lotta crunch, without a whole lotta mess. Serve these with Smashed Potato Salad with Green Goddess Dressing (page 76).

MAKE THE WINGS: Preheat the oven to 450°F (230°C). Line a baking sheet with foil and place a rack over the baking sheet. Spray the rack with cooking spray.

Thoroughly pat the chicken wings dry with a paper towel. In a large bowl, mix the baking powder, salt, and pepper and toss the wings until evenly and fully coated. Arrange the wings on the rack, allowing space between each wing.

MAKE THE SAUCE: In a small saucepan over medium-low heat, combine the gochujang, gochugaru, mayonnaise, vinegar, sesame oil, ginger, garlic, brown sugar, and honey and stir until the sugar is dissolved and the sauce is smooth, about 1 minute. Cover and set aside.

Bake the wings for 20 minutes. Before turning the wings over, brush both sides with sauce. Continue to cook until the wings are crispy, another 15 to 20 minutes.

Transfer the wings to a serving platter. Reheat the remaining sauce, drizzle the sauce over the wings, and top with toasted sesame seeds and green onion. Serve with cilantro jalapeño sauce alongside.

Chandani's CHICKEN TORTILLA SOUP

Serves 4

For the spice blend

- 2 teaspoons red chili powder
- 2 teaspoons ground cumin
- 1½ teaspoons garlic powder
- ½ teaspoon ground coriander
- ½ teaspoon smoked paprika
- ½ teaspoon onion powder
- ½ teaspoon dried oregano
- ¼ teaspoon freshly ground black pepper
- 1 teaspoon salt

For the soup

- 1½ pounds (680 g) boneless, skinless chicken breasts
- 2 tablespoons unsalted butter
- 5 cloves garlic, minced
- 1 onion, finely diced
- 1 (10-ounce/280 g) can diced tomatoes and green chiles (I like Rotel)
- 7 cups (1.7 L) chicken broth
- Juice of ½ lime
- ¼ cup (10 g) finely chopped fresh cilantro
- ¼ cup (15 g) thinly sliced green onions
- Salt and freshly ground black pepper

Toppings

- Diced avocado
- Chopped fresh cilantro
- Sliced jalapeño chiles
- Shredded Monterey Jack or cheddar cheese
- Tortilla strips
- Sour cream

I love a good tortilla soup. And while I've made many versions over the years—roasting tomatoes and onions, rehydrating pasilla peppers to get their authentic and deeply aromatic flavor infused in the broth—this easy version that my cousin Chandani makes is just as flavorful without all the extra work! A variety of spices are simmered with the broth and the chicken, imparting their rich aromatics. I add slices of creamy avocado to balance out the spicy rich broth, along with favorite toppings like shredded cheese and tortilla strips for a fully satisfying meal.

MAKE THE SPICE BLEND: In a small bowl, combine the chili powder, cumin, garlic powder, coriander, paprika, onion powder, oregano, black pepper, and salt and mix well.

MAKE THE SOUP: Place the chicken on a plate and evenly coat both sides of the breasts with the spice blend. You will have some leftover to add to the pot later with the chicken.

In a dutch oven or large pot, melt the butter over medium-low heat. Add the garlic and onion and cook until the onion is soft and translucent, 4 to 6 minutes.

Increase the heat to medium and add the chicken breasts. Cook for 6 to 7 minutes on each side, lowering the heat if needed so the spices do not burn. Add the remaining spice blend, the diced tomatoes and green chiles, and the broth and stir, using a wooden spatula to scrape up any brown bits from the bottom of the pot.

Bring the soup to a boil, cover, lower the heat, and simmer for 20 minutes, stirring occasionally.

Using a slotted spoon, remove the chicken breasts, and allow them to cool for a few minutes. Shred the chicken with your fingers or two forks into bite-size pieces and return the chicken to the pot. Add the lime juice, cilantro, and green onions. Season with salt and pepper to taste. Serve immediately with the toppings.

CBLT
& CURRY AIOLI

Serves 4

1 pound (455 g) bacon

1 teaspoon red chili powder

1 teaspoon ground coriander

1 teaspoon tandoori masala

½ teaspoon freshly ground black pepper

½ cup packed (110 g) brown sugar

1 cup (240 ml) Curry Aioli (page 256)

8 slices good-quality sandwich bread

8 Bibb or other soft lettuce leaves

2 large tomatoes, sliced

Salt and freshly ground black pepper

Sweet and spicy candied bacon and a delicious curry aioli take a basic BLT from good to GREAT! I love this on sourdough, because that's just my personal obsession, but pillowy soft potato rolls or brioche would be perfect choices, too. Be sure to make extra bacon, because anyone in the vicinity of the kitchen will try to steal a piece! Leftover curry aioli can be used in a wrap with some rotisserie chicken for a quick curry chicken salad vibe.

Preheat the oven to 375°F (190°C). Place a wire rack over a foil-lined baking sheet.

Arrange the bacon on the wire rack. In a small bowl, mix the chili powder, coriander, tandoori masala, pepper, and brown sugar. Evenly distribute the sugar and spice mix among the bacon slices and gently press so it adheres to both sides of the bacon.

Bake the bacon until the brown sugar is melted and the bacon is crisp, 25 to 30 minutes, turning the bacon midway through baking. Remove from the oven and allow the bacon to cool on the wire rack.

Assemble the sandwiches by spreading 2 tablespoons curry aioli on each slice of bread, and then build the sandwiches by layering the lettuce, tomato slices (lightly sprinkled with salt and pepper), and bacon between two slices of the bread. Repeat with the remaining bread and fillings. Cut each CBLT in half and serve.

ORECHIETTE

with SPICY SAUSAGE KHEEMA & KALE

Serves 4

- 2 teaspoons fennel seeds
- 1 teaspoon cumin seeds
- 2 teaspoons coriander seeds
- 4 black peppercorns
- 2 tablespoons extra-virgin olive oil
- 2 cups (220 g) diced onion
- 1 pound (455 g) spicy Italian sausage, removed from the casings and broken into small pieces
- 1 tablespoon minced garlic
- 1 teaspoon crushed red pepper, plus more for serving if desired
- 1 teaspoon garam masala
- ¾ pound (340 g) Tuscan kale, center ribs removed, leaves coarsely chopped (about 3 cups)
- 1 pound (455 g) orecchiette pasta, cooked according to package directions and kept warm
- 1 cup (240 ml) pasta cooking water, reserved
- ¾ cup (70 g) grated Pecorino Romano, plus more for serving
- Salt
- 8 to 10 fresh basil leaves, finely chopped

Pasta with kale and sausage is elevated to new heights with this rockin' spice blend. The entire dish comes together with a generous amount of my favorite cheese, Pecorino Romano, which I would eat on pretty much anything! This pasta also invites all sorts of swaps—try using ground beef, lamb, or chicken instead of the sausage, or sub in spinach for the kale. For a fully vegetarian version of this dish, replace the sausage with white beans or chickpeas.

Toast the fennel, cumin, coriander, and peppercorns in a dry skillet over medium heat until fragrant, watching carefully so they do not burn. Let cool slightly, then transfer to a spice grinder and pulse until finely ground; set aside.

In a dutch oven or large high-sided skillet (big enough to hold the pasta with a fitted lid), heat the oil over medium. Add the onion and cook for 3 to 4 minutes, stirring occasionally, until slightly translucent. Add the sausage and cook for 3 to 4 minutes, and allow the meat to brown.

Stir in the garlic and crushed red pepper and cook until the garlic is fragrant but not brown, about 1 minute, reducing the heat if necessary.

Add the toasted spice blend and garam masala to the pan and stir to combine. Reduce the heat to low, add the kale, and cover. Add the cooked orecchiette, ½ cup (120 ml) of the reserved pasta water, and the Pecorino Romano and stir well to combine. The sauce is done when the kale is wilted and the mixture is creamy. If it is dry, slowly add the remaining ½ cup (120 ml) pasta water.

Taste and adjust for salt, add the fresh basil, and serve the pasta with more cheese and crushed red pepper if you want additional heat.

PRO TIP

If you don't have the whole spices called for in this recipe on hand, you can use already ground spices and lightly toast them for a similar effect.

LAMB CHOPS

with CHIMICHURRI COUSCOUS & GARLICKY YOGURT SAUCE

Serves 4

- ⅓ cup (75 ml) extra-virgin olive oil, plus more for finishing
- 1 teaspoon salt, plus more if needed
- ¼ teaspoon freshly ground black pepper, plus more if needed

  Juice of ½ lemon
- 8 rib lamb chops, or one rack of lamb, cut into chops

  Chimichurri (page 257)
- 2 cups (360 g) cooked couscous or orzo, warmed
- 1 cup (240 ml) Garlicky Yogurt Sauce (page 260)
- 3 tablespoons finely chopped fresh parsley, for garnish
- 1 tablespoon finely chopped fresh mint, for garnish

  Lemon wedges, for serving

PRO TIP

Always bring meat just about to room temperature before cooking so you get an immediate nice sear.

This is a special-occasion dish if ever there was one! I love a good, simple lamb chop served with a zesty chimichurri. It's my go-to order at a steakhouse. Here, the lamb and couscous soak up the puckery flavors of the chimichurri and the yogurt sauce, and everything comes together in unison in that very first bite. Chimichurri is the perfect way to use up any extra fresh herbs lying around, so feel free to play around with the recipe based on what you have on hand. The sauces and couscous can be made in advance so they'll be ready to go once the lamb leaves the pan.

In a small bowl, stir together ¼ cup (60 ml) of the olive oil, the salt, pepper, and lemon juice. Rub the marinade onto both sides of the lamb chops.

Heat a cast-iron pan or cooking pan with the remaining oil over high heat. When the pan is almost smoking, add the lamb chops and cook for 3 to 4 minutes per side. When meat is medium rare, a meat thermometer registers 120 to 125°F (48 to 51°C). Keep in mind that the lamb will continue to cook as it rests, so pull it earlier if you prefer it more pink and later if more well done.

Meanwhile, stir ¼ cup (60 ml) of the chimichurri into the couscous and season with more salt and pepper if needed.

Mound the couscous in the middle of a serving platter and arrange the chops around the couscous. Drizzle the chimichurri over the lamb and dollop the garlicky yogurt sauce between the chops and over the top of the couscous. Top with finely chopped parsley and mint, and serve with lemon wedges and a drizzle of extra-virgin oil.

SNACKS & DRINKS

If you follow me on @thechutneylife, you know that my favorite way to entertain is with a big spread of snacks, bites, and tasty cocktails, all at the ready as soon as guests walk in the door. It makes them feel welcome and quickly puts everyone at ease.

As always, I encourage you to not drive yourself completely bananas over making every single thing from scratch. Hosting is supposed to be FUN, so remember it's totally okay to mix and match homemade and store-bought apps, for both variety and ease. Serving most items at room temp means that the bulk of the work can be done well before guests arrive. It also means that you can enjoy some quality hangout time, instead of being stuck at the stove and sink!

When it comes to planning a menu, I like to have snacky, room-temperature bites out on the table for people as soon as they arrive. Next, I'll make one or two hot hors d'oeuvres and either put them out on the table or walk around offering them to guests because I'm a stickler for serving hot food HOT. I round out the offerings with some high-quality store-bought items, such as cheeses, olives, and a variety of breads, crackers, and veggies.

All of the dips in this chapter are great for a crowd and can easily be doubled or tripled. Serve them with crackers, pita triangles, sliced baguette, and interesting veggies.

When it comes to adult beverages, I'm a huge fan of making big-batch cocktails, forgoing the fussiness and mess that comes with making just a couple at a time in a cocktail shaker. It's so much easier to make a pitcher of something and pop it in the fridge the night before. The day of the party, guests can just pour right from the pitcher into their ice-filled glasses, add a splash of club soda or bubbly or whatever they prefer, then a garnish—and voilà! Done and done! This chapter offers four of my most widely loved cocktails.

When I developed these cocktail recipes, I wanted to avoid processed ingredients and sugar mixes as much as possible. Just real ingredients that get their flavor from a bounty of ripe fruit and herbs.

HERBED RICOTTA CROSTINI DIP

Serves 6

Jammy, roasted cherry tomatoes come together with herb-infused ricotta and a touch of heat, courtesy of serranos, in this addictive dip. Serve with lots of crusty sliced bread or crackers.

For the tomatoes

- ¼ cup (60 ml) extra-virgin olive oil
- 2½ cups (365 g) cherry tomatoes, halved
- 10 cloves garlic, thinly sliced
- 1 tablespoon crushed red pepper
- ½ teaspoon salt

For the ricotta mixture

- 1 (15-ounce/430 g) container whole-milk ricotta cheese
- 2 serrano chiles, roughly chopped
- ⅓ cup (15 g) finely chopped fresh cilantro
- ⅓ cup (17 g) finely chopped fresh parsley
- 10 fresh basil leaves
- 3 cloves garlic, peeled
- 1 teaspoon salt, plus more if needed
- 1 tablespoon extra-virgin olive oil

- Freshly ground black pepper
- 5 fresh basil leaves

MAKE THE TOMATOES: Heat the oil in a large skillet over low heat. Add the tomatoes, garlic, crushed red pepper, and salt and simmer for 8 to 10 minutes, until the tomatoes start to release their juices.

MAKE THE RICOTTA MIXTURE: In a food processor, combine the ricotta, serranos, cilantro, parsley, basil, garlic, salt, and oil and blend until smooth. Taste for seasoning, adding more salt if needed.

To assemble the dip, spread the ricotta on a large platter or serving dish and place the cherry tomato mixture on top. Add some freshly ground black pepper, top with more fresh basil, and serve.

HOT & *CHEESY* CORN DIP

Serves 6

2 tablespoons unsalted butter

1 tablespoon canola or vegetable oil

3 serrano or jalapeño chiles, finely diced

1 red bell pepper, diced

1 green bell pepper, diced

½ teaspoon salt

2 tablespoons minced garlic

1 bag (14.4 ounce/410 g) frozen corn, thawed and rinsed

1 tablespoon garlic powder

1 tablespoon ground cumin

2 teaspoons cayenne pepper

1 teaspoon dried oregano

1 teaspoon onion powder

2 tablespoons Cilantro Chutney (page 193)

1 cup (40 g) finely chopped fresh cilantro

1½ tablespoons sriracha sauce, or more to taste

¾ cup (180 ml) mayonnaise

⅓ cup (75 ml) milk

12 ounces (340 g) shredded Mexican cheese blend (about 4 cups)

Green onions

Pico de gallo

Chopped jalapeño chiles

Tortilla chips, for serving

I like to think of this dip as the one that put @thechutneylife on the Instagram map, along with my Cilantro Jalapeño Sauce (page 252). It's something I've made for family Christmases for years—aunts bring little Tupperware containers to fill with it and take home and enjoy. It's the dip I confidently recommend to everyone, from the most experienced home chef to the most nervous novice cook wanting to wow guests and make an impression. It's creamy, cheesy, and a total crowd-pleaser!

Preheat the oven to 400°F (205°C). Lightly oil a 9 by 9–inch (23 by 23 cm) or 9 by 11–inch (23 by 28 cm) baking dish.

Melt the butter and oil in a large skillet over medium heat. Add the serranos, red and green peppers, and salt and cook, stirring occasionally, until the peppers are softened, 5 to 7 minutes. Add the garlic and cook for 1 to 2 minutes, until fragrant but not browned. Add the corn, garlic powder, cumin, cayenne, oregano, and onion powder and stir to evenly combine. Continue to cook for about 8 minutes, stirring occasionally. Stir in the cilantro chutney, chopped cilantro, and sriracha and remove from the heat. Add the mayonnaise, milk, and all but ⅓ cup (40 g) of the shredded cheese and mix well.

Transfer to the prepared baking dish, cover with foil, and bake on the middle rack until bubbling, about 15 minutes.

Remove from the oven. Turn the oven temperature to low broil. Sprinkle the reserved ⅓ cup (40 g) grated cheese over the dip and broil for 1 to 2 minutes, until the cheese is golden brown.

Top with green onions and garnish with pico de gallo and jalapeños. Serve hot with tortilla chips.

QUESO *BLANCO* DIP

Serves 6

3 tablespoons unsalted butter

½ small onion, diced

4 jalapeño chiles, finely diced

2 teaspoons grated garlic

1 teaspoon salt

2 tablespoons all-purpose flour

1⅓ cups (315 ml) whole milk, warmed

2 teaspoons ground cumin

½ teaspoon cayenne pepper

¼ cup (60 g) chopped pickled jalapeño chiles, plus 2 tablespoons pickling liquid

¼ cup (40 g) finely chopped fresh cilantro

6 slices white American cheese

Salt and freshly ground black pepper

Tortilla chips, for serving

Even the cheese snob in me knows that for a queso to be truly velvety and delicious, some sort of processed cheese has to come into play. And I'm totally okay with that because this cheesy dip is one that people *always* love. Enjoy it with tortilla chips or crudités, or try it on the Kofta Subs (page 159).

In a medium saucepan or large skillet with high sides, melt the butter over medium-low heat. Add the onion, half of the chopped jalapeño, the garlic, and salt, and cook, stirring frequently, until the onion is soft and the garlic is fragrant, about 5 minutes. Add the flour and stir continuously until the flour begins to turn golden and nutty.

Reduce the heat slightly and whisk in the milk slowly, in small increments, to create a smooth sauce. Once you've incorporated all the milk, add the cumin, cayenne, half of the pickled jalapeños, the 2 tablespoons pickling juice, and half of the chopped cilantro. Add one slice of cheese at a time to the pot, whisking between each slice to blend the melted cheese into the sauce. Taste and season with salt and pepper.

Transfer to a bowl and top with the remaining chopped fresh jalapeños, pickled jalapeños, and cilantro. To keep warm, serve this queso in a plug-in fondue pot or a Crock-Pot. Serve with tortilla chips.

HOAGIE DIP

Serves 6 to 8

8 ounces (225 g) spicy capicola, cut into ¼-inch (6 mm) dice

8 ounces (225 g) Genoa salami, cut into ¼-inch (6 mm) dice

8 ounces (225 g) roasted black pepper–crusted turkey breast, cut into-¼ inch (6 mm) dice

8 ounces (225 g) white American cheese or Cooper sharp cheddar, cut into ¼-inch (6 mm) dice

1 small white or red onion, very thinly sliced

3 tomatoes, cored and chopped

1½ cups (360 ml) mayonnaise

Freshly ground black pepper

2 teaspoons dried oregano

Large pinch crushed red pepper flakes, plus more to taste

3 tablespoons extra-virgin olive oil

2 tablespoons red wine vinegar, plus more to taste

½ cup (120 g) prepared roasted Italian sweet peppers, drained and chopped

½ cup (120 g) prepared roasted Italian hot peppers, drained and chopped, plus more to taste

2 tablespoons pickled jalapeño chiles, chopped, plus 2 tablespoons pickling liquid

3 cups (165 g) shredded iceberg lettuce (from ½ small head)

6 (6-inch/15 cm) hoagie rolls, torn into 1-inch (2.5 cm) pieces

This dip, filled with pretty much everything you'll find in a good Italian hoagie (plus I added some turkey breast), brings back memories of years spent working in my family's deli. It was one of those corner stores that had been a neighborhood gem for almost fifty years, and when my parents needed help, I'd run the register, stock the refrigerator, or be summoned to the deli to wrap hoagies, slice meats, and take orders. I'd try just about anything from the deli case, and it's truly where my love of cold cuts comes from. For this dip, I would suggest going to your favorite deli and asking for meat and cheese in 8-ounce (225 g) chunks, rather than slices, as you'll be cutting everything into small cubes that you can scoop up with pieces of hoagie rolls. While Provolone is the cheese traditionally used in Italian hoagies, I prefer the milder American cheese. Hoagies are also a very personal thing, I totally get it, which is why I encourage you to adjust this recipe to your liking. You could add an extra splash of vinegar for more tartness, or toss in a handful of extra peppers for added heat. It's perfect to bring to a backyard barbecue or a potluck. Scoop, dip, and drip!

Mix all the ingredients except the rolls in a large bowl. Serve with hoagie roll pieces for dipping.

This dip is best served after it has had some time to really marinate in all the flavors, so make it the night before or refrigerate it for a few hours, then add the lettuce right before serving.

BARBECUE CHICKEN DIP

Makes 4 cups

1 tablespoon canola oil, plus more for the baking dish

½ small onion, finely diced

1 jalapeño chile, finely diced

2 teaspoons minced garlic

2 teaspoons ground cumin

1 teaspoon ground coriander

1 teaspoon garam masala

1 teaspoon red chili powder

½ teaspoon ground turmeric

¼ teaspoon salt

¾ cup (180 ml) prepared barbecue sauce (I like Sweet Baby Ray's)

2 tablespoons finely chopped fresh cilantro

8 ounces (225 g) cream cheese, softened

1½ cups (170 g) shredded Colby Jack cheese

½ cup (120 ml) ranch dressing, plus more for serving

2 cups (450 g) shredded rotisserie chicken

½ green bell pepper, finely diced

½ cup (30 g) sliced green onions

1 jalapeño chile, thinly sliced

Tortilla chips, for serving

I made this dip for my cousin Dev and his friends for a house party once, and they all went wild for it. It's one of those creamy, cheesy dips that you just can't go wrong with. I use a store-bought rotisserie chicken and a bottle of my favorite store-bought barbecue sauce for a quick hack that saves me a ton of time, allowing me to whip this up on short notice. For a vegetarian version of this dip, replace the chicken with pinto beans for a barbecue baked bean dip that's just as delicious!

Preheat the oven to 350°F (175°C). Lightly oil an 8-inch (20 cm) square baking dish or a 2-quart casserole dish.

Heat the oil in a saucepan over medium-high. Add the onion and jalapeño and cook for 2 to 3 minutes, until the onion has begun to soften. Reduce the heat to medium-low, add the garlic, and stir for about 1 minute, until fragrant, but take care not to burn it. Add the cumin, coriander, garam masala, chili powder, turmeric, and salt and cook for about 30 seconds. Add the barbecue sauce and cilantro. Stir to combine evenly and cook for an additional 2 to 3 minutes.

Remove the pan from the heat and add the cream cheese, shredded cheese, ranch dressing, shredded chicken, bell pepper, and half of the green onions.

Transfer the mixture to the baking dish and top with the jalapeño and remaining green onions. Bake until hot and bubbly, about 30 minutes. Serve hot with tortilla chips and extra ranch dressing on the side.

HUMMUS, *TWO WAYS*

Anytime I'm entertaining and want to make something quick but tasty and easy to leave out for guests to enjoy, I make hummus. Not only is it great as a dip with some veggies or pita, you can also make a big batch at the beginning of the week and use it on sandwiches, with roasted vegetables, in a bowl with some chicken, or even as a base on flatbread. Both of these versions make use of ingredients you already have in the fridge and pantry— and you can totally switch up the herbs or the amount of harissa you add, based on your preferences.

Cilantro Jalapeño Hummus

Makes 1½ cups (360 ml)

1   jalapeño chile, cored

¼   cup (10 g) roughly chopped cilantro (leaves and tender stems)

2   cloves garlic, peeled

2   teaspoons fresh lemon juice

2   tablespoons extra-virgin olive oil

¾   teaspoon salt

½   teaspoon ground cumin

3   tablespoons ice-cold water, plus more if needed

1   (15½-ounce/445 g) can chickpeas, drained and rinsed

In a blender, add the jalapeño, cilantro, garlic, lemon juice, oil, salt, cumin, ice water, and chickpeas and blend on high until smooth. Blend in additional ice water, if needed, to thin the hummus.

Harissa Hummus

Makes 1½ cups (360 ml)

1   (15½-ounce/445 g) can chickpeas, drained and rinsed

¼   cup (60 ml) harissa (I prefer Mina brand)

¼   cup (50 ml) tahini

2   tablespoons extra-virgin olive oil

½   teaspoon ground cumin

3   tablespoons ice-cold water, plus more if needed

1   teaspoon salt

In a blender, add the chickpeas, harissa, tahini, oil, cumin, ice water, and salt and blend on high until smooth and creamy. Blend in additional ice water, if needed, to thin the hummus.

TANDOORI ONION TART

Serves 6

1 sheet best-quality frozen puff pastry

1 cup (245 g) ricotta cheese

½ cup (55 g) grated aged Provolone or Parmesan cheese

½ cup (75 g) crumbled feta cheese

1 large egg

4 large cloves garlic, grated

2 tablespoons finely chopped fresh parsley

1 teaspoon dried Italian seasoning

¼ teaspoon salt

½ teaspoon freshly ground black pepper

Tandoori onions (see page 91)

Chopped fresh thyme or oregano, for garnish

PRO TIP

Defrost the puff pastry overnight in the fridge, or for an hour or so on the counter. Once thawed, the pastry should be easy to roll; if not, allow it to sit until it is pliable, but don't let it get too warm or it will become too difficult to work with and you'll lose the tender layers.

Flaky puff pastry, warm gooey cheese, and buttery tandoori onions—what's not to love? This savory, cheesy tart is the perfect app to serve as part of a bites buffet, as it can be prepped fully in advance and refrigerated for up to 8 hours before baking. I like to play with different cheeses for this recipe, but I always keep ricotta in the mix for the creamy factor. You can also turn these into mini tartlets by pressing small squares of the puff pastry dough into mini muffin tins. Double the recipe for the onions, if you like, and keep them on hand for my masala-spiced turkey burgers (page 91).

Preheat the oven to 400°F (205°C). Line a baking sheet with parchment or a silicone liner.

On a lightly floured surface, roll out the pastry into an 11 by 13–inch (28 by 33 cm) rectangle. Transfer to the prepared baking sheet and prick the dough all over with the tines of a fork to prevent the tart base from bubbling up.

In a medium bowl, mix the cheeses, egg, garlic, parsley, Italian seasoning, salt, and pepper. Spread the cheese mixture over the dough, leaving a ½-inch (12 mm) border. Brush the edges lightly with water, fold the sides of the dough over, and press them to create an edge, pinching the corners and pulling them a little away to make small points like the tip of a star.

Bake for 15 minutes, remove from the oven, top the cheese with the tandoori onions, and bake for an additional 10 to 15 minutes, until the cheese is golden and bubbly and the sides and bottom of the crust are golden brown (watch carefully to make sure it doesn't burn).

Let the tart rest for 1 minute and then using a pizza cutter, cut it into 2-inch (5 cm) squares. Sprinkle with fresh herbs and serve.

ACHARI-STUFFED MUSHROOMS

Serves 4 to 6

For the mushrooms

- 1 tablespoon extra-virgin olive oil, plus more as needed (or use nonstick cooking spray)
- 1 pound (455 g) baby bella mushrooms
- ¼ teaspoon salt
- Freshly ground black pepper

For the stuffing

- 4 ounces (115 g) cream cheese, softened
- 1 (4-ounce/115 g) jar pimento peppers, drained and chopped
- 4 green onions, thinly sliced
- ¼ teaspoon onion powder
- ¼ teaspoon garlic powder
- ½ teaspoon salt
- Generous pinch freshly ground black pepper
- 1 tablespoon extra-virgin olive oil or cooking spray
- 1 serrano chile, finely chopped
- ½ cup (65 g) finely chopped red onion
- 2 cloves garlic, finely chopped
- ½ teaspoon Italian seasoning
- 2 tablespoons finely chopped fresh cilantro

For the topping

- 2 teaspoons extra-virgin olive oil or cooking spray
- ¾ cup (60 g) panko breadcrumbs
- 1 clove garlic, finely chopped
- 2 teaspoons achar masala
- 2 tablespoons grated Pecorino Romano cheese

Listen, I know how overdone stuffed mushrooms are as a party app, but if I see them being served, I can't help but reach for one. This recipe calls for achar masala, which is generally used as a pickling spice for pickled mango and can be found at South Asian markets or online. When I was growing up, I enjoyed it on everything from garlic bread to boiled eggs, and it's super delicious on sliced cucumbers. You could also make this more of a meal by using large portobello mushrooms and adding cooked crumbled sausage to the cream cheese and pimento mixture. If you're serving these for a party, you can make and refrigerate the stuffing up to 2 days ahead. You can also freeze these appetizers on parchment paper in a small, carefully wrapped pan. When ready to serve, cook them from frozen in a preheated 400°F (205°C) oven for 30 to 40 minutes, depending on the quantity.

Preheat the oven to 400°F (205°C). Line a baking sheet with foil. Place a baking rack on top of the foil and brush or lightly spray with oil.

MAKE THE MUSHROOMS: Remove the mushroom stems and reserve. Using a small spoon or the opposite end of a spoon, scoop out the flesh, taking care not to break the caps. Roughly chop the stems and flesh and set aside.

Place the mushroom caps on the prepared baking sheet. Lightly brush them with the 1 tablespoon olive oil, and season with the salt and pepper to taste.

Bake the mushroom caps for 5 to 7 minutes, until they are slightly browned and softened. Set aside the mushroom caps, still on the baking sheet. Do not turn off the oven.

MEANWHILE, MAKE THE STUFFING: In a medium bowl, mix together the cream cheese, pimento peppers, green onions, onion powder, garlic powder, salt, and pepper.

Heat a large skillet over medium-high heat and add the oil. Once the oil is hot, add the serrano and let sizzle for about 10 seconds, and then add the onion and garlic and cook until the onion is translucent, 5 to 7 minutes. Add the mushroom stem and flesh mixture and Italian seasoning and cook until the mushrooms are soft and the liquid has been absorbed. Add the cilantro and mix well. Transfer to a bowl and let cool slightly. Once cool, add to the cream cheese mixture and blend well. Refrigerate for 30 minutes.

MAKE THE TOPPING: Heat the oil in a skillet over medium-high heat. Add the breadcrumbs and garlic and toast until the panko is golden, stirring frequently, 1 to 2 minutes, reducing the heat so the garlic doesn't burn. Transfer to a bowl and stir in the achar masala and Pecorino Romano.

Fill each mushroom cap with a heaping teaspoon of stuffing, then add the panko topping. Bake until the topping is golden, about 20 minutes. Serve warm.

PRO TIP

To clean the mushrooms, use a vegetable brush or dry/damp paper towel—you do not want to wash them as they will absorb too much water and be soggy.

POBLANO NACHOS

with CHORIZO

Serves 6

1 tablespoon canola or vegetable oil, plus more for the baking sheet

1 pound (455 g) ground chorizo

2 teaspoons taco seasoning

1 teaspoon red chili powder

1 teaspoon ground cumin

1 (14-ounce/400 g) bag tortilla chips

1 (14-ounce/400 g) can black beans, drained and rinsed

1½ cups (360 ml) fresh store-bought salsa or pico de gallo

1½ cups (360 ml) poblano cream sauce (page 142), ¼ cup (60 ml) reserved

1 pound (455 g) shredded Mexican cheese blend

⅓ cup (40 g) Cotija cheese

⅓ cup (15 g) roughly chopped fresh cilantro (leaves and tender stems)

1 small red onion, thinly sliced, for garnish

2 radishes, thinly sliced, for garnish

1 lime, cut into wedges, for serving

Warning: These nachos with chili, chorizo, and poblano cream sauce are *addictive*! Truthfully, I'm a sucker for even simple cheese and beans nachos, but when you want to elevate them, making them with my rich and creamy poblano sauce (see page 142) adds so much flavor. While these are in the snacks section and perfect as a party app (think game day for sure!), I love a tray of these on the coffee table to enjoy for dinner as we watch our favorite show. The chorizo and beans make these nachos hearty and filling; to make them vegetarian, skip the chorizo and double the beans. If you can, try to purchase thicker tortilla chips that can stand up to all the toppings!

Preheat the oven to 375°F (190°C). Line a large baking sheet with foil and lightly brush or spray with oil.

Heat the canola oil in a large skillet over medium-high heat. Add the chorizo, taco seasoning, chili powder, and cumin and cook until the meat is browned and cooked through, 5 to 6 minutes. Remove the meat to a colander over a bowl to drain off any excess fat.

Spread one-third of the tortilla chips in a layer on the bottom of the prepared baking sheet. Layer one-third of each of these ingredients in the following order: the chorizo, beans, salsa, poblano cream, and shredded Mexican cheese. Repeat the layers in this order two more times, ending with the shredded cheese.

Bake in the preheated oven until the cheese is bubbling, 15 to 20 minutes.

Spoon the ¼ cup (60 ml) reserved poblano cream sauce over the nachos and sprinkle with the Cotija and cilantro. Top with the onion and radishes and serve with the lime alongside.

Mom's
MASALA CASHEWS

Makes about 2½ cups (340 g)

1   teaspoon black salt

1   tablespoon red chili powder

¾   teaspoon freshly ground black pepper

½   teaspoon salt

2   cups (480 ml) canola or vegetable oil

12   ounces (340 g) cashews

PRO TIP

Work in batches to toss the hot cashews with the spice mix right when they come out of the oil so the spices really adhere.

My mom usually makes these savory spiced nuts around the holidays, when unannounced visitors are bound to pop in and she needs to make sure the snack cabinet is stocked and ready to go. They're made with a simple spice blend of black salt, red chili powder, and black pepper, so every ingredient counts. Black salt is distinctive and offers an important flavor. It comes together with the chili powder and the black pepper to create more than the sum of its parts. I highly recommend making a trip to a South Asian market to find it, or looking online. It's just not right how quickly these nuts disappear in my house!

In a small bowl, stir together the black salt, chili powder, pepper, and salt. Divide the spice blend between 2 large heatproof bowls.

Heat the oil in a heavy-bottomed medium pot over medium-low until it registers 350°F to 375°F (175°C to 190°C) on a candy or deep-fry thermometer. Add half the nuts and fry for about 30 seconds. Carefully remove with a slotted or mesh spoon and toss the nuts in one bowl of the spice blend to coat. Repeat with the remaining batch, coating the nuts in the second bowl of the spice blend. Let cool and serve. Nuts can keep for up to a week in the refrigerator or stored in a tin in the pantry.

ROSÉ SANGRIA *SURPRISE*

Serves 6

1 bottle (750 ml) rosé

4 ounces (120 ml) vodka

Juice of 2 lemons

2 ounces (60 ml) elderflower liqueur (St-Germain)

8 strawberries, hulled and sliced

2 peaches or red plums, sliced

½ cup (60 g) fresh raspberries

¼ cup (60 ml) agave

San Pellegrino or club soda (optional)

I love a refreshing sangria, but not one that's laden with a ton of juice. Instead, I prefer adding loads of fresh fruit to rosé and letting it all sit overnight, so the rosé takes on both a beautiful color and just the right amount of fruitiness. I like to control the sugar content by adding as little or as much agave as I choose, so feel free to play with that. Every sip reminds me of summer, and a little kick from the vodka makes this more cocktail-like than just a glass of rosé. A few edible dried rose petals as a garnish or edible flowers in ice cubes make for a gorgeous drink!

In a pitcher, mix together the rosé, vodka, lemon juice, elderflower liqueur, strawberries, peaches, raspberries, and agave. Let sit in the fridge for about 2 hours, or overnight. When ready to serve, pour into big, round wine glasses filled with ice, add a splash of sparkling water to each, if desired, and serve with straws.

GIN-GER & TONIC

Makes 8 drinks

8 ounces (240 ml) Cardamom-Ginger Simple Syrup (recipe below)

8 ounces (240 ml) gin, preferably Hendrick's

8 ounces (240 ml) fresh lime juice

16 ounces (480 ml) tonic water

8 sprigs fresh rosemary

PRO TIP

Garnishes aren't just for looks. The aroma of a sprig of rosemary as you sip your cocktail adds to the flavor you experience; often I swap the rosemary for Thai basil or a sprig of thyme—be fancy, and don't forget the garnish.

Who doesn't love a gin and tonic, and especially one that's elevated with fresh ginger! This cardamom-ginger simple syrup is something I make in big batches and keep in the refrigerator to add to just about any drink—it is DIVINE. (You can replace the sugar in my Pineapple Mojitos [page 190] with this syrup for something more fun.) This cocktail comes to the rescue for last-minute dinner guests, or when Pinank and I just need a nightcap after a long week. I usually have most of the ingredients on hand.

Add the syrup, gin, and lime juice to a large pitcher and stir to combine well. Keep in the fridge until ready to serve. Pour into individual glasses filled with ice, about three-fourths of the way full, and top with a splash of tonic water. Garnish each with a rosemary sprig.

CARDAMOM-GINGER SIMPLE SYRUP

2 cups (400 g) sugar

15 green cardamom pods, slightly crushed with the back of a spoon

½ cup (50 g) sliced fresh ginger

In a saucepan, combine the sugar, cardamom, and ginger with 2 cups (480 ml) water and bring to a boil over medium-high heat. Reduce the heat and simmer for 8 minutes. Let cool, and then strain through a fine-mesh sieve, discarding the solids.

CHUTNEYS & CONDIMENTS

While this chapter may be at the back of the book, the recipes inside it are the true heroes of any recipe. When it comes to cooking, I am all about the sauce.

Chutneys and condiments elevate any dish and any meal. Most of the items in this chapter can be used interchangeably, with anything from a stuffed veggie sandwich or scrambled eggs to grilled vegetables or a roast chicken. They are the workhorses of any kitchen, and I encourage you to experiment with them in as many ways as possible.

Most of the recipes in this chapter are the first thing I knock off on my prep list. When you prepare your sauces and condiments in advance, you are ahead in the meal-prep game. I encourage you to pick three of your favorite recipes from this chapter and make them at the beginning of the week. Keep them in squeeze bottles in the fridge and use them in both expected and unexpected ways. Try Athela Marcha (page 264) on a bagel with cream cheese, or Chaat Onions (page 260) with whatever vegetable or meat you may be grilling.

Traditionally there are four chutneys used for chaat: Cilantro Chutney (page 193), Yogurt Chutney (page 194), Spicy Garlic Chutney (page 195), and Tamarind Date Chutney (page 195)—and they all come together to make a dish that is spicy, sweet, savory, and tangy! Making all of these at once may feel time-consuming, but I always make them a day or two before I plan to use them, and sometimes even a couple weeks ahead and freeze them, which makes prep the day of so much easier.

CILANTRO JALAPEÑO SAUCE

Makes ¾ cup (180 ml)

2 jalapeño chiles, 1 seeded, both halved

1½ cups (60 g) roughly chopped fresh cilantro (leaves and tender stems)

3 cloves garlic, peeled

2 tablespoons freshly squeezed lime juice

½ cup (120 ml) mayonnaise

1 teaspoon ground cumin

PRO TIP

Making this in a high-speed blender will turn the texture and color into something that is a little too neon green, so I highly recommend using a mini food chopper or food processor for best results.

This is the OG *Chutney Life* sauce and has been a fan favorite since the early days of my blog. An all-purpose condiment to keep in your fridge at all times. Use it as a dip for some frozen samosas, drizzle it over your favorite Mexican dishes, use it as a base for chicken salad—there are a hundred applications you'll want to try. If you're looking for a lighter version, you can swap the mayo for plain Greek yogurt, and for a vegan version, replace regular mayo with vegan mayonnaise. While this recipe uses jalapeños, they can be finicky in their spice level, so taste and increase to your heat preference, or use a serrano to really kick it up!

In a small food processor or mini food chopper, combine the jalapeños, cilantro, garlic, lime juice, mayonnaise, and cumin and blend until smooth. Refrigerate for up to a week.

APPLE BUTTER CHUTNEY

Makes 1 cup (240 ml)

1 cup (240 ml) prepared apple butter

¼ teaspoon black salt

¾ teaspoon ground cumin

¾ teaspoon red chili powder

Sugar to taste, if needed

This Apple Butter Chutney is a quick hack to use in place of the traditional Tamarind Date Chutney (page 195) for Chaat (page 183) and other recipes. One thing to note is that apple butter can vary in consistency and sweetness, so taste and adjust as needed. Your finished product should be sweet, slightly tart, and have just a little bit of spicy kick. In chaat and other dishes, the sweet chutney helps balance the spicy, herby cilantro and yogurt chutneys that are traditionally used together as a trio of chutneys. You are looking for a spreadable consistency, so you may need to add a few tablespoons water if your apple butter is very thick. Black salt has a smoky, pungent, mineral-like taste, similar to sulfur, and I encourage you to try it in this recipe; otherwise you can replace it with chaat masala for a similar taste.

In a small bowl, whisk together the apple butter, black salt, cumin, and chili powder. Add sugar for sweetness, if needed, and add water, 1 tablespoon at time, as needed, to create a spreadable consistency. Refrigerate for up to a week.

CHIPOTLE AIOLI

Makes ¾ cup (180 ml)

½ cup (120 ml) mayonnaise

½ cup (20 g) coarsely chopped fresh cilantro

2 canned chipotle peppers in adobo, plus 1 teaspoon adobo

1 tablespoon honey

½ teaspoon ground cumin

1 jalapeño chile, coarsely chopped

1 tablespoon apple cider vinegar

2 cloves garlic, peeled

½ teaspoon crushed red pepper

This creamy, smoky, spicy chipotle mayo with a hint of honey is perfect as a dip for quesadillas, on top of a fried egg, or spread inside a panini. It's sweet, spicy, and tangy all in one!

In a small food processor or blender, combine the mayonnaise, cilantro, chipotle peppers, adobo, honey, cumin, jalapeño, vinegar, garlic, and crushed red pepper. Blend until smooth. Refrigerate for up to a week.

PRO TIP

Leftover canned chipotle peppers can be frozen in a plastic container and added to soups, stews, and salsas for extra spice and smokiness.

COCONUT CILANTRO CHUTNEY

Makes 1½ cups (360 ml)

- ½ cup (20 g) chopped fresh cilantro (leaves and tender stems)
- 1 cup (85 g) frozen shredded coconut
- 2 serrano chiles
- 1 tablespoon peeled and grated fresh ginger
- 2 tablespoons chana dalia
- ¼ teaspoon salt
- 1½ tablespoons canola oil
- 1 teaspoon mustard seeds
- ¼ teaspoon hing (asafetida)
- 2 teaspoons urad dal
- 4 to 5 curry leaves

I love coconut chutney with dosas and uttapam (see page 165), and this version incorporates cilantro, which gives it an additional layer of flavor and also a gorgeous color. Chana dalia, which is chana dal husked, split, and roasted, and frozen coconut (both can be found at your local Indian store) lend a coarse texture to this chutney, so be sure to not over puree it! While this is traditionally served with uttapam, it would also be excellent paired with the Asparagus & Pepper Jack Rosti with Tarragon Garlic Aioli (page 42) or as a dipping sauce for Coconut Shrimp Po' Boys with Panang Curry Remoulade (page 206).

In a small blender, combine the cilantro, coconut, serranos, ginger, chana dalia, salt, and ½ cup (120 ml) water and blend until fairly smooth in texture (this is not meant to be silky smooth, but rather a bit thick). Add additional water if needed, 1 tablespoon at a time. Transfer to a bowl.

Heat the oil in a small pot over medium-high. Once the oil is hot, add the mustard seeds, hing, urad dal, and curry leaves. When everything begins to crackle and pop, mix the toasted spices and dal into the coconut chutney. Keep in the fridge in an airtight glass container for up to 5 days.

AIOLI, *THREE WAYS*

Curry Aioli

Makes 1¼ cups (300 ml)

Try this as a dressing for chicken or egg salad, or as a spread in sandwiches and wraps!

1   cup (240 ml) mayonnaise

½   teaspoon red chili powder

3   large cloves garlic, grated

1½   teaspoons curry powder

½   teaspoon garam masala

1   serrano chile, finely chopped

¼   cup (15 g) chopped fresh cilantro (leaves and tender stems)

In a small bowl, mix together the mayonnaise, chili powder, garlic, curry powder, garam masala, serrano, and cilantro. Refrigerate for up to a week.

Tarragon Aioli

Makes 1½ cups (360 ml)

I try to always keep some of this aioli on hand in the fridge, because there's pretty much nothing I won't eat as long as I have this herby goodness on top or alongside. It's my mid-afternoon snack with some baby carrots and cucumber spears, or my base for a crudités platter. Additionally, serve it with grilled or roasted veggies, and try it with grilled meats. This is a no-fail condiment!

1   tablespoon Dijon mustard

2   tablespoons extra-virgin olive oil

1   cup (240 ml) mayonnaise

2   cloves garlic, grated

     Zest from 1 lemon plus 2 teaspoons lemon juice

2   tablespoons finely chopped fresh tarragon

In a medium bowl, lightly whisk the mustard, oil, mayonnaise, garlic, lemon zest and juice, and tarragon until well combined. Refrigerate for up to a week.

Sriracha Aioli

Makes ½ cup (120 ml)

This condiment is similar to Japanese spicy mayo. It's a quick and easy way to add heat and flavor to sandwiches. Try topping off fried or grilled veggies with a dollop, or serve alongside fritters or french fries.

½   cup (120 ml) mayonnaise

2   tablespoons sriracha sauce, or more to taste

¼   teaspoon ground cumin

In a small bowl, whisk together the mayonnaise, sriracha, and cumin until smooth. Refrigerate for up to a week.

CHIMICHURRI

Makes 2 cups (480 ml)

1 cup (50 g) finely chopped fresh parsley leaves

⅓ cup (15 g) finely chopped fresh cilantro leaves

2 tablespoons fresh oregano leaves

¼ teaspoon crushed red pepper

1 shallot, coarsely chopped

2 cloves garlic, finely grated

1 red Fresno chile, finely diced

½ teaspoon ground cumin

2 tablespoons red wine vinegar

1 teaspoon salt

½ teaspoon freshly ground black pepper

¾ cup (180 ml) extra-virgin olive oil

If you ask me what's really on rotation in my kitchen during any given week, it starts with chimichurri. Especially when I have an excess of herbs on hand, since you really don't want to take any shortcuts here: Don't replace the fresh herbs with their dried versions. Drizzle this on grilled chicken, roasted veggies, or toss it with some chopped cherry tomatoes for a chimichurri bruschetta situation—the sky is the limit. It's bright, packed with fresh herbs, and so delicious. And if you're grilling, it's great on everything from fish and shrimp to steak and lamb chops!

In a medium bowl, add the parsley, cilantro, oregano, crushed red pepper, shallot, garlic, red chile, cumin, vinegar, salt, black pepper, and oil and whisk to combine. Store in a tightly covered jar in the refrigerator for up to a week.

TZATZIKI

Makes 1¼ cups (300 ml)

2 Persian cucumbers

Salt

1 cup (240 ml) full-fat plain Greek yogurt

2 tablespoons finely chopped fresh parsley

1 tablespoon finely chopped fresh dill

1 tablespoon finely chopped fresh mint

1 tablespoon fresh lemon juice

1 tablespoon extra-virgin olive oil

2 cloves garlic, minced

2 teaspoons salt

Freshly ground black pepper

This traditional, creamy Greek yogurt–based sauce is a favorite with grilled vegetables, chicken, and meat. It's also perfect as a dip for vegetables or crackers.

Grate the cucumbers on the large holes of a box grater, sprinkle with a pinch of salt, then let sit for about 10 minutes in a colander to drain the excess liquid.

In a medium bowl, add the yogurt, parsley, dill, mint, lemon juice, oil, garlic, salt, and pepper to taste and mix to combine.

Gently squeeze any remaining liquid from the cucumbers and stir the shredded cucumbers into the yogurt mixture. Refrigerate for at least 1 hour before serving. It will keep for up to 3 days.

CLASSIC RAITA

Makes 1½ cups (360 ml)

3 Persian cucumbers

1 small carrot, peeled and finely grated

2 Thai green chiles, finely chopped (use 1 if you prefer less spice)

¼ cup (25 g) chopped fresh cilantro

1 cup (240 ml) whole-milk plain yogurt

¼ teaspoon rai na kuria (ground mustard seeds)

½ teaspoon salt

¼ teaspoon black salt or ½ teaspoon chaat masala

⅛ teaspoon red chili powder

⅛ teaspoon freshly ground black pepper

Pinch sugar

¼ teaspoon ground cumin

PRO TIP

If you plan on making this in advance, be sure to make it just a couple hours ahead of time. If it sits too long, the carrots and cucumbers will release too much of their liquid, making the raita watery.

Raita is a yogurt-and-cucumber-based condiment known for its ability to balance the heat from spicy curries and rice dishes like biryani. I always spoon raita right next to whatever curry I'm eating, as I love the juxtaposition of flavors when it hits my tongue. Hot, cool, tart—all of it! There are SO many variations of raita, but I appreciate a dependable classic recipe like this one. Aside from eating it with traditional meals, raita makes a great dip for a crudités platter. Rai na kuria (ground mustard seeds) add a peppery flavor unique to raita; if you have extra you want to use up, it's also used in Athela Marcha (page 264). You can find rai na kuria at South Asian markets or online, or take whole mustard seeds and use a mortar and pestle to grind them.

Shred the cucumber on the small holes of a box grater. Use your hands to squeeze out the excess water and discard it. Put the cucumber in a medium bowl and add the remainder of the ingredients. Stir to combine well. Let sit for about 30 minutes to allow the flavors to meld, then serve.

CHAAT ONIONS

Makes about 1 cup (125 g)

1 large Vidalia onion, halved and sliced ⅛ inch (3 mm) thick

¼ teaspoon red chili powder

½ teaspoon salt

¾ teaspoon ground cumin

1½ teaspoons fresh lemon juice

¼ teaspoon chaat masala

2 tablespoons finely chopped fresh cilantro

I grew up eating raw onions as a side salad to most traditional Gujarati meals, and now it's so hard to eat a dish like Mom's Dal Fry & Jeera Rice (page 180) without them!

In a small bowl, add the onion, chili powder, salt, cumin, lemon juice, chaat masala, and cilantro, mix to combine, and serve immediately.

Garlicky YOGURT SAUCE

Makes 2½ cups (600 ml)

2 cups (480 ml) full-fat plain Greek yogurt

3 cloves garlic, grated

2 tablespoons finely chopped parsley

1 teaspoon salt

1 teaspoon crushed red pepper

3 tablespoons fresh lemon juice

¼ cup (60 ml) extra-virgin olive oil

Feel free to up the garlic, boost the lemon, add more herbs—this sauce is a canvas for your creativity. It's great with lamb chops and grilled fish, or as a sub for tzatziki when you just want something quick and easy. Let this sit for at least an hour before serving, to develop flavor.

In a small bowl, whisk together the yogurt, garlic, parsley, salt, crushed red pepper, lemon juice, and oil. Refrigerate for up to a week.

LASANYU MARCHU

Makes ¾ cup (180 ml)

65   cloves peeled garlic (about 1¼ cups/180 g cloves from 6 to 7 heads)

1½   teaspoons salt

½   cup (65 g) red chili powder

A staple ingredient in almost all Gujarati households is lasanyu marchu. Copious amounts of garlic and red chili powder get pounded together in a medium-size mortar and pestle (or work in batches if using a smaller one) until a thick paste forms. It sounds like a heavy hitter, but think of it as a concentrate that can be added to things like cream cheese or mayo to make a garlicky spread. It's what gives Breakfast Naan Pizza (page 35) and Barbecue Paneer Pizzas (page 88) that delicious kick. My mom mixes it with a bit of peanut oil and salt to enjoy with leftover paratha and her morning chai. I've also added a tiny bit to soups or pastas when it needs a little extra heat! Try it mixed into cream cheese and spread onto bagels, topped with cucumbers and tomatoes; mixed into mayo as a spread for sandwiches; thrown into a pot of spaghetti; or just spread on top of some toasted naan as a snack.

Add the garlic and salt to a large mortar and pound with the pestle until the cloves begin to break down and form a paste. Add the chili powder, a few large spoonfuls at a time, and continue to pound and grind after each addition. Use a spoon to scrape down the sides of the bowl as needed, until a thick paste forms.

Or, add all the ingredients to a food processor and pulse, scraping down the sides of the bowl, until a thick paste forms. Place in a sealed glass container and refrigerate until ready to use, for up to 3 months.

ATHELA MARCHA

Makes 1 generous cup (about 250 ml)

1 tablespoon rai na kuria (ground mustard seeds; see headnote, page 259)

2 tablespoons canola or vegetable oil

½ teaspoon salt, plus more if needed

½ teaspoon ground turmeric

¼ teaspoon hing (asafetida)

¾ teaspoon fresh lime juice

4 large jalapeño chiles, sliced into ⅛-inch (3 mm) rounds

Enjoy these pickled jalapeños with mustard seeds on tacos, on bagels with cream cheese, as a side to almost anything, really! These jalapeños are best marinated overnight and eaten within 4 to 5 days; refrigerate them to maintain their crispness and freshness.

Using a spice grinder, pulse the crushed mustard seeds into a coarse powder. If you don't have a spice grinder, you can use a mortar and pestle, or place the mustard seeds in a ziplock bag and use a rolling pin to crush them.

In a large, wide, glass-lidded bowl or jar, add the oil, crushed mustard seeds, salt, turmeric, hing, and lime juice and stir to combine.

Add the jalapeños and mix thoroughly to evenly coat the jalapeño slices with the spices and oil. Taste and adjust for salt (depending on the size of your jalapeños, the amount of salt needed can vary). Place the lid on the bowl and refrigerate overnight before serving.

Acknowledgments

You guys, the procrastinator and self-doubter in me cannot believe I wrote a frickin' cookbook!

To the readers and followers of *The Chutney Life* who have supported me over the years with likes, comments, and shares, and who have made my recipes through times of joy, times of sadness, and everything in between; and your DMs, filled with praise and love about how a recipe reminded you of your mom's cooking, or helped you finally impress your skeptical in-laws, or, better yet, got your picky toddler to finally eat something other than chicken nuggets: Thank you for rooting for me and reminding me constantly that my food, and my story, is worthy of space on the shelf.

I have many people to thank for helping me create this book. Here are just a few of them:

Andrea Barzvi, I'm so grateful for the pep talks, the genuine guidance, and the help whenever it was needed, throughout the entire cookbook process.

Ali Wald, it couldn't have been easy to keep track of a million moving pieces, but you juggled it all like a pro. Thank you for being in my corner!

The fabulous team at Abrams, including Holly Dolce who guided me so effortlessly with her accomplished expertise while also giving me the space to carry out my vision for this book. Monica Shah, for believing in me without ever having met me—you are a gem of a human, and I will be forever grateful for this opportunity.

Pamela Cannon, for dealing with my hot mess self with so much patience, but mostly for putting my voice and sentiments into words that a human being can comprehend (not easy with jibber-jabber and procrastination). I dreaded the writing of this book, but you made it feel so effortless and so me. You are a force!

Lauren Deen, for not only testing the recipes, but for the million trips to South Asian markets all over NYC that filled your pantry with dozens of spices. Your spot-on opinions and honest advice were invaluable.

The amazing styling team of Tammy Hardeman, Abby Gaskins, and Lily Kaplan who approached TCL with so much commitment, working on every recipe and photo until it was perfect while still keeping the process fun. You gave it your all—thank you, thank you!

Emily Dorio, you turned my home upside down for a few days for our photo shoot, but you approached it all with so much grace, kindness, and imagination. Every day I could see the tiny little sparks firing in your brain to make the photographs in this book as perfect as possible. Thank you for everything you did to make this collection look and feel more special than I could ever have imagined!

Kalpana Aunty, for the long hours in the kitchen, making sure everyone was fed and happy, and for being such an amazing team player. All of it required so much grit, and you never so much as let out a sigh of exhaustion. Your energy is unmatched.

My parents, whose care and attention toward those they love in the form of food and joy I carry with me. In times of celebration, in times of grief, when words fail, you've taught me the magic a meal can make. I'm constantly humbled by how much you give, and how you never falter in helping others. I am blessed to be yours.

Chandani and Dev, your bickering and eye-rolling know no bounds, but you keep it real and approve only the best recipes! I truly cannot imagine a life (or a book) without you in it. You are my anchors, and the best Masi and Mama.

Pinank, aka Mr. Chutney Life, for doing and being all the things I cannot. You are the true definition of a partner—unwavering and unrelenting in encouraging me to achieve all my dreams. I love you so much, but please don't reference this book when I ask you what you want for dinner.

And lastly, the two brightest lights in my life, Shaan and Sahil. Of all the titles I've held and will hold, my favorite will always be Mommy.

Index